Some Kind of Wise Guy

SOME KIND OF
WISE GUY

Stories about parents, weddings, modern living, and growing up Italian

Bill Ervolino

Record Books

Published by
Record Books
150 River Street
Hackensack, NJ 07601

Distributed by
Koen Book Distributors
P.O. Box 600
Moorestown, NJ 08057

First published in 1997 by Record Books,
a division of The Bergen Record Corp.

"Nightmare Before Christmas" and "Bald Like Me" originally appeared in *Long
Island's Nightlife* and are reprinted here with the permission of publisher Michael
Cutino.

ISBN: 0-9654733-2-5
CIP Data available

10 9 8 7 6 5 4 3

PRODUCED BY K&N BOOKWORKS INC.
TEXT AND COVER DESIGN BY PATRICE SHERIDAN
AUTHOR PHOTOGRAPHS BY CARMINE GALASSO

Printed in the United States of America

For Emilio and Louise, of course

But that's okay. I'm no prize package, either.

This collection, consisting of my own personal favorites, should give you a reasonable enough glimpse at them and me.

A few of the stories are about important events in my life, but the bulk of them are about the simple everyday things that drive most of us crazy, told in what I've come to think of as the easy conversational style of a dyed-in-the-wool, born-again wise guy.

I hope you enjoy reading them as much as I've enjoyed writing them.

And if you don't ... oh, I don't know ...

Go to Hollywood.

An Italian Family

The Wonder Years

In less than five months I'm going to be the same age my parents were when I started high school.

This is significant.

For the last year or so I've been telling myself that turning forty wasn't going to be a big deal for me. What difference could it possibly make?

"Hi, my name is Bill. I'm thirty-nine."

"Hi, my name is Bill. I'm forty."

Who cares?

But when I look at my parents I realize it does make a difference, because I still think of *them* as being forty.

Psychologists say this isn't unusual. Children tend to freeze their parents at a certain age, even though the practice can be emotionally stunting, and often requires several rolls of wax paper.

It's also disorienting.

"Oh, what's the matter?" my father asked last weekend. (I knew I didn't wrap that wax paper tight enough.) "You think you're not gonna be cool anymore? Me and your mother are almost seventy, and we're still cool."

"Dad, trust me. You're not cool."

"Well, your cousin Caroline said we're cool. We've got the *Tony Bennett Unplugged* album."

"Dad, your undershirt is sticking out of your fly. You're not cool. Forget about it."

"Here," he said, tossing the Tony Bennett CD to me. It hit me in the head, and all of a sudden, everything started spinning ... spinning ... *spinning.*

The next thing I knew, it was 1969. The summer after the summer after the Summer of Love. And everything was just the way it was twenty-six years ago!

Oy.

The mists clear. My father is working for a company called Graybar Electric. He has sideburns. He wears fat ties and flared pants and brushes his teeth—Oh my God, he still has teeth!—with Ultra Brite. (Yeah, keep brushing, Dad. It's not gonna make any difference.)

He thinks he looks cool. He thinks he dresses cool. In fact, he thinks he's so cool he could pass for thirty. But The Beatles have just broken up and he still doesn't know which one is which.

"Bill, hurry up! One of The Beatles is on Merv. I think it's Bingo."

My mother has just gotten a job at the new Alexander's in Valley Stream. They assign her to Young Misses, which, after a few short months, is transformed into the Feelin' Groovy department.

Whenever I call her at work she answers the phone by saying, "Feelin' Groovy, Louise."

"Hi, it's me." Feelin' Groovy Louise's son.

The sadists who redesigned this house of horrors dimmed the lights, attached a mirrored ball to the ceiling, and installed black Plexiglas room dividers all over the place.

Every night, all these tired old matrons lugging shopping bags come through the department to get out to the parking lot, walk smack into the Plexiglas, and just about kill themselves. My mother then runs to the phone, calls security, and yells into the receiver, over the trippy din of Cream singing "Sunshine of Your Love."

There's been another dark surprise in Groovyland.

My mother is wearing black boots, a blue velour midi-skirt with a bolero vest, and a white turtleneck draped with strands of thin gold chains. She comes home around 6 P.M. and she's still making dinner when my father walks in, half an hour later, and starts undoing his big fat tie.

My friend Lenny, in the throes of puberty, is staying for dinner. In the living room he whispers, "You know, your mother's not bad lookin' for a woman her age."

"Lenny, don't make me throw up."

"And your father's pretty cool for an old guy. *Nice tie, Mr. Ervolino!*"

"He can't hear you in the bedroom," I explain. "Tell him at dinner."

Lenny asks me if I think my father fools around, and I start laughing. "Who'd fool around with him? He's forty."

"Really?" Lenny asks. "I thought he was younger. Must be the sideburns. *Nice sideburns, Mr. Ervolino!*"

"Thanks, Lenny," my father says, walking past us into the kitchen where the veal cutlets are crackling in the pan. Within seconds, my brother flies in through the side door and heads straight to the bathroom to wash his hands.

I roll my eyes. "Lenny, you're like the only person I know who can actually have conversations with old people."

My mother shouts, "Dinner's ready!" and places the cutlets on the table, alongside a bowl of corn, a bowl of potatoes, a big bowl of iceberg lettuce, and three bottles of Kraft salad dressing: French, Russian, and Roka.

"Hey," Lenny tells me, as we walk out of the living room, "we're all gonna get old sooner or later."

And so we did: me ... my brother ... Lenny ... Tony Bennett ... Even Bingo.

Fully Armed, We Hit the Beach

I went to the beach last weekend because I had spent the previous two weekends locked in my apartment, sitting in front of the AC, taking cold showers, and waiting for fall. By Saturday the walls were closing in.

The beach offered me the chance to sit in traffic, soak up dangerous ultraviolet rays, immerse myself in foamy brown water, listen to forty-three very loud radios (tuned to forty-three different stations), and eat ... ugh ... frankfurters. (I'm not sure which part of which animal is used to make frankfurters, but I have a sneaking feeling you could cut out whatever part it is and the animal would continue walking around and never miss it.)

At the stroke of 6, I trudged home, sat in front of the AC, took cold showers, and waited for fall.

Is it hot out there or is it me?

To be honest, the beach has never appealed to me much. When I was a kid my parents took my brother and me to Jones Beach just about every weekend, and it was a production number of mythical proportions.

In the parking lot, I'd see these cute little blond families pop out of their station wagons and scamper off toward the sand. The big blond daddy would have this little tote bag filled with suntan lotion, and the big blond mommy would be carrying a kerchief, and they'd rent chairs and umbrellas, buy hamburgers and Cokes, and watch their little blond button noses turn golden brown.

My family wasn't like that.

For starters, my mother would cook for three days: potatoes and eggs, peppers and eggs, eggplant parmigiana; there was no end to it. We'd bring a big silver cooler that weighed about six hundred pounds, a thermos that weighed another forty, two dozen rolls, twelve loaves of Italian bread, peaches, plums, nectarines, cherries, assorted condiments, nuts, nutcrackers, forks, spoons, knives, napkins, towels, sheets, blankets, pillows, pillowcases, suntan lotion, floats, inner tubes, iodine, bandages, a complete change of clothes for each one of us, books, newspapers, magazines, two aluminum patio chairs, a chaise lounge, our own umbrella, pails, shovels, power tools ...

It would have been easier to go to the beach, dig up the sand, and bring it home.

I'd stare in wonder at the families who could actually go to the beach without taking so much as a pair of sunglasses. They'd run off to rent all their junk while we'd have to stop halfway through the parking lot to catch our breath.

It took us half an hour just to unload the trunk and figure out how we were going to haul it all in one trip. My brother and I were loaded up like pack mules while my father fumbled with the cooler, the umbrella, and anything else he could hold. My mother, meanwhile, ran shopping bags up her arms like bangle bracelets.

"This hurts," I said, one hazy, hot, and humid morning, referring to the chaise lounge strapped to my back. "It's hitting me in the head."

"We're almost there," my mother yelled. "Don't spill the gravy."

I had a big plastic bag in one hand and a big paper bag in the other. Both arms were numb to the elbow. My brother was holding so many things I couldn't even see him. He looked like a float in the Lawn Furniture parade.

When we finally hit the sand we had to help my father set everything up. The umbrella had to be twisted, turned, and pushed into the ground until it was stationary.

"This will only take a minute," he'd say, but it always took about twenty.

Once the umbrella was up, we'd lay the blanket down under it, place the cooler on top of it, arrange the chairs neatly around it, set up the lounge chair perpendicular to it, hang the sheets from the umbrella to block the wind ... it was like building the Little House on the Prairie.

"Where would you like the piano, lady?"

And when we were done, we ate—whether we wanted to or not.

ME: Let's go in the water.

MOTHER: Have some eggplant first.

ME: It's too hot. All the other kids are in the water.

FATHER: Pass the sauce.

MOTHER: I don't know why I make all this food. It's so much work. I was up at six o'clock this morning ...

BROTHER: I want a hot dog.

MOTHER: I'll break your legs.

ME: Let's go in the water.

MOTHER: What's with this bread?

FATHER: They were out. I had to go to the other place.

ME: Can we go swimming now?

MOTHER: You just ate. You'll get the bends and get carried out to sea. Have a cherry; they're sweet as sugar.

ME: I don't want a cherry. I want to go in the water.

MOTHER: Does this bathing suit make me look fat?

FATHER: I'm ready for a nap.

ME: I'm having a horrible time. Everyone's looking at us.

MOTHER: Why would they look at us? Come with me to the water fountain so I can wash the pots.

A Full House

In the heartwarming afterglow of turkey, stuffing, carrots, turnips, baked potatoes, mashed potatoes, sweet potatoes, and potato cro-quettes—my family is a walking "stop the insanity" commercial—the Ervolinos inevitably sit down to play cards: blackjack. Poker. Acey-deucey. Seven-card stud. No-peekie baseball.

Dealer's choice.

The participants: my father. My mother. My uncle Ziti. My aunt Mafalda. My uncle Rotelle. My widowed aunt Philomena. And my crazy old aunt Putana, who's ninety-three and still greets me by grab-bing me below the waist even though I've told her sixty times that if she does it again I'm going to hit her with a mop.

Even though all of us have already spent three hours eating and making small talk, it isn't until we begin to play that I realize half of them can't hear, the other half can't see, and none of them can remember anything that happened the day before yesterday.

"OK, folks," I say, "seven card. Ten cents up."

Like clockwork, Rotelle turns to Ziti and squints. "What'd he say?"

"Seven card," Ziti yells. "Put in a dime."

I give everyone their first two cards down, check mine, then deal the first of the open cards, calling them out as I go. "Seven. Queen. Big ace. Three of clubs. Deuces never loses. Another queen. Ace bets."

Nothing.

"Ace bets."

Nothing.

"Aunt Mafalda! Ace bets!"

"Oh! That's me? What do I do?"

She's been asking this same question in every card game since the Nazis invaded Poland. I tell her to put a dime into the pot.

"Another one? OK."

She smiles and throws in a dime. The rest of us do the same.

I deal the second round of open cards: "Five. Ace-king. Pair of threes! Four of hearts ..."

Things are cooking. Then suddenly: trouble.

PHILOMENA: I told you Cookie had a stroke?

ME: Threes bet.

PUTANA: Who? Cookie who?

PHILOMENA: Cookie that was married to Sal the plumber, may he rest in peace.

ZITI: Sal from the old neighborhood?

ME: Threes bet. Come on, people.

MOTHER: No. I know who he means: Fat Sal the Plumber. No, she's talking about Junie's sister Cookie, from North Sixth Street.

PUTANA: Cookie who?

PHILOMENA: Yeah. Junie. Junior. Chubby's husband, may she rest in peace. You remember. Junie moved into his mother-in-law's may she rest in peace's house, when Cookie was living next door.

ZITI: I knew them?

PHILOMENA: Sure. You used to go to Aqueduct with Junie and Sal and the other one, the cab driver may he rest in peace with the thing on his nose. I forget his name. My legs are killing me today. Who bets?

ME: Threes bet. Uncle Rotelle.

ROTELLE: Oh. Me? How much?

PUTANA: Are you talkin' about Cookie with the big head?

ME: Ten cents.

ZITI: I have to go to the bathroom.

ME: Already?

MAFALDA: It's his prostate.

MOTHER: Who wants coffee?

FATHER: I'm ready.

ME: Ma, come on. We just started playing.

MOTHER: Well, I'll put it up. Your father wants coffee. Who wants coffee?

MAFALDA: I'll have some.

MOTHER: Black or brown?

MAFALDA:	If you're gonna make black, I'll have black. I think I have a flush.
ME:	How can you have a flush?
ROTELLE:	No, that's good! A flush is good!
MAFALDA:	Well, I think I have one.
PHILOMENA:	Show me. I'll tell you.
MOTHER:	Who wants black and who wants brown? Billy, put the chestnuts on the table. Who wants chestnuts?
ME:	No! There'll be shells all over the place.
MOTHER:	Maybe they're hungry.
ME:	How could they be hungry? They've been eating for three hours! They'll explode.
MAFALDA:	See? I do have a flush. Should I bet a quarter?
ME:	You can't have a flush! You only have four cards!
MOTHER:	Stop yelling! Why do you have to yell at everybody?
ME:	Because they're all deaf, that's why!
MOTHER:	Nobody's deaf. It's Thanksgiving. Anyway, there's chestnuts for later, Philomena's pastry, and all those cookies.
PUTANA:	Cookie who? Cookie from Brooklyn?

Shopping with Emilio and Louise

My parents arrived last weekend for their second visit in four years. (Be still my heart.) In her hands was a box of cannolis. In his was a box of fifty or so tomatoes, from his garden, individually wrapped in newspaper.

"What's this?" I asked, skimming the headlines.

"That's so they won't ripen all at once," he told me. "Every morning while you're having your coffee, open them up and see which ones are ripe. The ones that are ripe, you can eat. The ones that are still green, wrap up again and put them back in the box."

"I see."

The man has totally lost his mind.

After lunch I washed the dishes and was about to make some coffee, when my mother said, "Did you get any half-and-half for your father?"

I told her I'd forgotten. "But it's no problem," I said, "the store is right around the corner. I have to get a few things anyway. It'll take ten minutes."

"OK," she said. "We'll come with you."

With me?

"Don't be silly," I told her.

She insisted, "We've never gone food shopping with you. Right, Emilio? It'll be fun."

The next thing I knew we were in the world's largest El Dorado, driving two miles an hour to the A&P. People were honking at us, screaming, throwing rocks. I slumped in the backseat and covered my eyes.

"Don't you listen to them," my mother told my father over the blare of the car horns. "You're going fast enough."

People on crutches were passing us. When we finally made it into the parking lot, the car jerked so many times I had to open the window and take deep breaths.

"Park right there," my mother said. "Oh, no. There's a cart. Try over there. No, it's too small. Over there. Someone's pulling out. No, she's pulling in. How about that one over there? No, over there. Go left. I mean right. Over there! Hurry!"

It was like astronaut training school.

Inside the store, things got progressively worse. Even if I'm doing a whole week's shopping I can be in and out in minutes. I know exactly what I want, exactly where it is, and I have the whole thing down to a science. My mother picked up everything in my cart, examined it, and replaced it with something else, until I finally rapped her knuckles with an eggplant.

In the cookie aisle, she reached into her pocketbook and pulled out her coupon file, which opened like an accordion. I thought she was going to play "Back to Sorrento."

"Oh, this is good," she said, handing me some cockamamie cake mix. "It only takes about two hours."

"Ma," I said, putting it back on the shelf, "I have a lot to do this week. I'm very busy. I have tomatoes to unwrap. Some other time."

My father, meanwhile, had taken off on his own, searching for bargains. He returned five minutes later with a plastic bag containing twenty-four rolls of toilet paper. "You use toilet paper," he asked, "don't you?"

"No, Dad. I live in the trees now with the monkey people."

"Well, this is a real deal," he said, stuffing it into my cart.

"I don't want a deal," I replied, handing it back to him. "I just want to get the hell out of here."

We finally made it to the checkout counter, wandered through the parking lot, and sputtered home.

We forgot the half-and-half, of course, but it never would have survived the trip.

The Bachelor Party

On July 22, 1955, my father became a father when my mother gave birth to me. I was born in Jamaica Hospital shortly after midnight and that's all I'm going to tell you because no one ever believes the part about the star and the wise men or the bluebirds who fluttered outside my mother's window and spelled out the name "Billy."

At the time of my birth, I had a head the size of a walnut, and I looked suspiciously like six pounds of chicken cutlets. In one early photo, my father is sitting on the living-room sofa, cradling me in the palms of his hands like the Allstate man, and my mother is sitting to his right, holding a bag of bread crumbs.

I spent a good deal of my early years trying to destroy that photo. I didn't think it was a very flattering shot because I was so scrawny and wrinkly and looked absolutely nothing like the paragon of manhood I have since become.

I'd see the photo every so often, usually on holidays when someone had the urge to pull the photos down from a shelf in the closet. But it took me several years before I could stop concentrating on what I looked like and began noticing my father, with that endearing cute/proud look on his face.

That I resembled six pounds of chicken cutlets was of little concern to him. I was *his* six pounds of chicken cutlets.

And when my brother came along three years later, I was naturally pleased that my father referred to us as Number One (me) and Number Two (my brother), phrases other families used only when they had to go to the bathroom.

As I blossomed into toddlerhood my father and I were always together. He taught me about art and music and a love for nature and animals. Many was the time he'd run to me in the backyard with a newspaper in his hand and say, "These are the names of all of the nice horseys who need money. Pick the ones you'd like to help and I'll go down to the track ... uh, the stable ... and see how much they need."

"Sure, Daddy! Should we ask Mommy to pick some too?"

"No, Son. Mommy's busy. Besides, it's better to do good works quietly, without seeking compensation, acknowledgment, or personal rewards. Although, if your picks are as good as they were last week, I may break down and buy a convertible."

My father never drank or ran around. In fact, except for an occasional spree at Aqueduct, he was kind of a goody-two-shoes. But in 1972, when we moved to Long Island, he became good friends with our thirty-five-year-old next-door neighbor Richard, who had "bad influence" written all over him.

I smelled peer pressure.

In 1974, when my father was forty-seven, he and Richard planned a bachelor party for Richard's brother-in-law, Mike, who was about twenty-nine at the time.

Naturally, the wives became all upset, as wives tend to do when the subject of bachelor parties comes up. But my father, who hadn't attended one of these functions in twenty years, was eager to be involved, and my mother eventually gave her blessing. So he went.

I was going to college and working nights at the time, and when I came home that night—actually 5:30 in the morning—I found my father in the den watching TV, reading a book, and looking suspicious. I asked how the party had gone.

"Oh, you know, good, good, we went here, went there, had a nice time, this and that, got home awhile ago, can't sleep, so I thought I'd sit around, catch up on my reading, oh, look, the sun's coming up, so how are you, how was work, what's new?"

I walked over to him and peered into his glasses. "Dad, I've had a very long night," I told him. "Please don't tell me you're on speed."

"Speed? Speed? Who said anything about speed? What's speed? What are you talking about?"

"Did anyone give you a pill?"

"Well ..." He turned away. I could tell he was embarrassed.

"I'm not going to yell at you, if you tell me the truth," I said. "What color was it?"

"Pink."

I started yelling. "You took a pink? Who gave you a pink?"

"Michael. I was falling asleep and he said it would wake me up. I didn't know what it was. Everybody was taking one."

"Oh and I suppose if everyone jumped off a bridge, you'd do the same thing?"

"I swear to you, I didn't know what it was, and I'm never going to do it again. Just, please, don't tell your mother; she wouldn't understand."

Of course she wouldn't. She only does downers.

"OK, Dad. Just hang on. I'm going to make you a sandwich."

"I'm not hungry."

"Dad, I'm making you a sandwich and you're going to eat the whole thing, and then try to get some sleep. Do you understand?"

"Uh, well, I don't know ..."

"Just say yes."

"Yes."

I could have been harsher with him, I suppose. Taken away his allowance. Grounded him for a week.

But he seemed so repentant and helpless and ... oh, I don't know. What can I say?

He looked just like 175 pounds of chicken cutlets.

Fried.

The Discount

Finally, the words I've been longing to hear: My mother's thinking about getting a job.

Work!

Something to keep her off the the streets!

I've been praying for this day ever since she retired.

Louise Ervolino is back in the job market.

Well, not officially. Not yet. But she's thinking about it. That's a start, right?

She's contemplating. That's a step in the right direction, isn't it?

She's got the bug. That's encouraging, wouldn't you say?

So now what do I do? Drop little hints? Renew her subscription to *Working Woman*? Pick up some subliminal tapes?

"Louise, go back to work ... Louise, go back to work ..."

The impetus for all this? Retirement, she says, has left her bored, empty, unfulfilled. She has nothing to do but cook, clean, stare at my father—"Have you ever taken a *good* look at him?" she asked me recently—and talk about the same six or seven relatives, over and over again.

"If I don't get out of this house, I'll go crazy," she insisted. "Maybe I'll go back to Stern's, or Macy's, or ..."

Suddenly, I got a twinge—one not unfamiliar to the children of mothers in retail—and a flashback: I'm nineteen years old, sitting in the kitchen, and my mother walks in, holding a dress.

"Did I show you my new dress?" she asks. "Guess how much I paid for it!"

"I don't know."

"Guess!"

"I don't know."

She rips off the belt and slaps the table like a whip. *"Guess!"*

"Uh ... I don't know ... $50? $40? $20? $90?"

And then it begins: "It was $85, marked down to $70, then it was marked down to $62. *And with my discount* it was $49. That's practically half price."

"That's great, Ma."

I'm sitting in the living room. A blouse enters.

"Guess how much I paid for this?"

I have no idea.

"It was $32, marked down to $27, then it was marked down to $21. *And with my discount* it was $16. That's practically half price."

"Ma, that *is* half price. Congratulations."

I'm pulling out of the driveway. In the rearview mirror I see my mother, glassy-eyed, teeth clenched, poised like a matador, waving a blue pleated skirt.

Over the roar of my engine, she screams, "Guess how much I paid for this?"

"Leave me alone!"

"Guess!"

I jump out of the car and run down the street. She runs after me. "It was $38 ..." she screeches.

Sweat pours from my brow. My heart is racing. I can't get away.

"Then it was marked down to $23.99!"

Someone help me, please!

I hop a fence. She hops it after me.

"Then it was marked down to $18!"

Help!

I crash to the pavement. Everything is spinning. She jumps on top of me, pins me down, and dangles the skirt menacingly.

"And with my discount ... guess how much it was? Guess! Guess! Guess!"

I can't take this anymore! I don't know! "It was $7! It was $4! It was free! They owe you money! I don't know! Leave me alone!"

"Guess!"

Aahhh!!!

The flashback ends with a close-up of my face and my lips mouthing a word: "retire."

The end.

(NOTE: Originally, this was a much longer flashback. But with my discount ...)

Tee for Two

My brother is turning on me.

No, really.

My brother, the grease monkey from Queens, is standing in the backyard of his sprawling suburban manse hitting a bucket o' balls.

Say it isn't so, Serpico.

"Hey, there," he says as I walk through the sliding glass doors onto his deck.

Hey, there?

Should I laugh? Should I cry? This *is* a joke, isn't it?

"No," he tells me. In fact, he played nine holes on Saturday. "It takes a long time," he explains.

I look into his eyes to make sure he isn't on anything. But he isn't. My brother has somehow, some way, for some reason, taken up golf.

Is this possible?

Ervolinos don't play golf. They play stickball. They bowl. They bocci. They pick tomatoes and take long naps.

When we were kids, we played miniature golf once in a while. That was fun. I really loved that windmill. And I always wound up with the highest score.

But *real* golf? That's for people who drink Dubonnet, own stock portfolios, and have children named Thurston, Huxley, and Gwendolyn.

Still, I'm careful not to overreact. Maybe it's just a phase. "So … uh … when did *this* start?" I ask as his club slices through the air.

"Last year," he tells me. "I took lessons when I was in Puerto Rico."

Well, that makes sense, I think to myself, conjuring up the names of all those famous Puerto Rican golf champions.

As the small white ball flies across the lawn, his labrador Sam dashes across the lawn to fetch it and bring it back to him.

"Want to give it a try?" my brother asks, handing me his club.

"Well … gee … I don't know … I mean …"

"Here! Try it! It's fun!"

Hmm ...

I put the ball down on one of those small plastic things, grasp the club, yell "Tally-Ho!" and ... you know ... gash up the lawn and miss the ball completely.

"No, no, no," my brother tells me through a mushroom cloud of grass and peat moss. Then he walks over and explains how I have to lock my fingers together and do a bunch of other stupid junk I can't remember.

My parents, meanwhile, are inside the house, staring at us through a window with a strange mix of suspicion and fear, as if two extraterrestrials had just landed in the backyard and were eating all the citronella candles.

At the conclusion of my mini lesson, I somehow managed to hit the ball over the back fence—no small feat. Naturally, I was thrilled. There's nothing quite like actually being good at something—even if you don't know what the hell you're doing.

Of course, my next few shots were less successful: I hit a tree, the side of the shed, the back of the dog's head. And I'm sure that must have hurt because he spent the rest of the afternoon walking backward.

Without Sam to retrieve the balls, the novelty wore off pretty quickly.

"Yeah," my brother said, "I'm getting kind of bored too. Maybe we should play some tennis ..."

Tennis? My brother plays *tennis*?

"Sure! I'll be right back!"

As he ran inside to get his rackets, I sat by myself on the deck, dazed and confused, rubbing Sam's head.

"Weird day," Sam said.

And getting weirder.

No Gifts, Please

Three years ago I decided to put all the birthday insanity behind me with two little words, and they weren't "Happy Birthday."

No gifts.

Understand?

No gifts.

I told my friends, my relatives, my immediate family … everyone I knew: no shirts. No pants. No socks. No jocks. No slippers. No ties. No dice.

And as long as we were on the subject: no brics, no bracs, no knicks, no knacks, no this, no that, no nothing.

Keep it. I don't want it. I don't need it, I can't use it, I have no place to put it. And I don't want to buy you anything, either.

My mother, of course, was the first to go into a kamikaze lolla-palooza nosedive: "What do you mean? What are you talking about? Birthdays are wonderful! Birthdays are special! Birthdays are …"

"Look," I said, "I have nothing against birthdays. I just don't want any gifts. And I don't want to buy any gifts. Anymore. Ever again."

Eventually, compromises were reached. My friends and I all agreed that on our birthdays we would take each other out to dinner. Period. My relatives also liked the dinner idea, either in a restaurant or in someone's house. Plus—you know there had to be a plus—$50 in cash to do whatever you wanted with.

Period.

OK. I can live with that.

And so in September, I gave my father $50, and my brother gave him $50, and we all went out to dinner.

In February, I gave my mother $50, and my brother gave my mother $50, and we all went out to dinner.

So far, so good.

But in July, everything fell apart. My brother Donald's birthday is July 10 and mine is July 22 and we all went out to dinner on the Saturday in between. I gave him a card with $50 in it, and he gave me a card with $50 in it, and my parents gave each of us $100.

I objected. "You're only supposed to give us $50," I said.

My mother disagreed. "It's $50 each," she told me. "You give me $50 and you give your father $50, so we give you $100. If you want us to give you $50, then just cut us in for $25, and we'll double the money back to you."

She sounded like Jimmy the Greek.

"This is ridiculous," I said. "Our birthdays are too close. You're going for $200 in one shot. It's too much."

"Don't worry about it. Eat your meatballs before they get cold."

Last year was even worse. At the beginning of July my mother called to tell me that my brother's girlfriend Joyce was going to make our "combined" dinner at Donald's house on the Sunday between our birthdays.

I showed up at 2 P.M., she made a great dinner, we blew out the candles, and then all hell broke loose. I gave my brother a card with $50 in it, my parents gave me a card with $100 in it, and my brother gave me a card with $100 in it.

"What's this?" I asked him. "Why did you give me $100?"

He was confused. "I thought we decided last year that we were raising it to $100."

I started rubbing my head. "That's not what we decided. We decided that Mom and Dad could give us $100 because we give them $50 each. You and I are supposed to give each other $50, too. I'm not taking $100 and just giving you $50."

You realize, of course, how moronic this all is. We could have just passed a wet teabag around the table and still wound up with the same amount of money in our pockets.

"Oh. Well … I don't know … keep it," he said. "I already gave them $100 for their birthdays. It doesn't make any difference."

"What are you talking about?" I turned to my parents. "Did he give you $100 each?"

My parents froze. My father said he didn't remember. "But what's the difference? He makes more than you. He can afford it."

"I don't believe you people!" I said, boiling. "I owe you $50 each." So I took the $100 my brother gave me and I gave it to them, and took another $50 from my wallet and gave it to my brother.

"Don't be silly," Joyce said, trying to be diplomatic. "Why don't you just consider the $100 as $50 from him and $50 from me, and we'll call it even?"

I thought it over for a second. "Well ... I suppose that'd work," I said to Joyce. "When's your birthday?"

"It was last month," she told me.

"Last month? And nobody said anything to me? What's *with* you people?"

So I took the $50 I gave my brother and gave it to Joyce, and then I took the $100 my parents gave me and gave it to my brother.

But Joyce said she couldn't accept it because then I'd wind up with nothing. "And it's your birthday," she said.

So she took the $50 I gave to her, passed it across the table to my mother, and told my mother to give it to me, which my mother did, along with another $100 to make up for the $100 she and my father gave me, which I had given to my brother.

This must have gone on for another twenty minutes until I had something like $600,000 in my lap and became so unglued I threw it all into the middle of the table and told everybody to just take what they wanted.

"And that's it!" I yelled. "Stop it! End it! I can't stand this anymore!"

Two weeks ago, my mother called with a suggestion.

Gifts.

The Big (Hot) One

My fortieth birthday has come and gone. And what started out as one of those quaint little "just us" get-togethers at my brother's house last Sunday quickly escalated into just us, and just my aunt Irene, and just a few cousins and friends.

Of course, that was fine with me. My brother and Joyce have a nice big house on Long Island, with a nice big central air-conditioning system.

What better way to spend your birthday, in the middle of summer, with the temperature hovering somewhere around … gee, what was it … 170 degrees?

I arrived about twenty minutes late because of the traffic, and my back was soaking wet, and my temples were throbbing like Donna Summer's *Bad Girls* album.

There were eight cars in the driveway when I pulled up, and I walked right through the garage and into the TV room, where I found no trace of anyone. I called out and no one answered, so I trudged into the dining room, where this wonderful, icy blast of air hit me in my hot, sweaty face. God, that felt great. Then I looked out onto the deck, where I saw my brother and everyone else standing around waving at me. Outside. In the sun.

This is a joke, right?

My mother came up to the door, shouting "It's the birthday boy!" Then once she was close enough, she whispered, *"We're having it outside. Don't say anything."*

I closed the door on her foot and said, "Fat chance, babe. I'm not leaving this house for love or money."

So she kicked the door open and gave me a great big kiss, and said, "Happy birthday! *Your brother bought a canopy for this party and all new lawn furniture, and he had the goldfish pond landscaped, and you're coming outside or I'll break your legs.*"

And I kissed her back and said, "Thank you! *I'm dripping with sweat, and I can't breathe, and I've been sitting in traffic for three hours, and there's no way in hell I'm going to …*"

Before I could finish, she grabbed my shirt, pulled me out the door, slammed it shut, and rolled a planter filled with geraniums in front of it. The next thing I knew everyone was walking over, kissing my sweaty cheeks, shaking my clammy hands, and asking if I wanted some iced tea.

Crud.

It was obvious that I wasn't the only one who was uncomfortable. My friend Danny was frantically fanning himself with a paper plate, and my cousin Frankie was splashing ice water on his chest, and when Joyce came out of the house with a big, cold bowl of potato salad, my poor, delirious father stuck his face in it and didn't come up for air for five whole minutes.

Throughout all of this my mother was doing her Queen of Denial bit, hopping from table to table and saying how beautiful the new canopy looked, and how sensational the new lawn furniture was, and how lucky I was to have such beautiful weather on my birthday.

"Well, it could be a little cooler," my aunt Irene said, just before her head burst into flames.

"No, it's perfect," my mother said, tamping out the fire. "If you're hot, sit under the canopy. Isn't it lovely? And did you see how nice the pond looks? I'll bet those goldfish are keeping nice and cool!"

"Ma," I said, "the goldfish are dead. If that water was any hotter you could boil spaghetti in it."

At one point Joyce seemed concerned. "Are you sure you don't want to go inside? It's really hot out here."

But before we could grab our plates and run for cover, my mother assured her that we were fine. And besides, she said, my brother was about to start the barbecue.

Just what this party needs: hot coals.

While the steaks and sausages were cooking my father started crying for no apparent reason, my cousin Anthony began wandering around the yard because he was certain he saw a giant bottle of Budweiser, and I picked up a fork and started scratching out my will on the tablecloth.

When I yelled out, "Does anybody want my stereo?" my cousin Frankie yelled back, "Is it cold?"

Then just when it seemed as if we were all doomed, the sky suddenly turned dark and it started to rain.

Rain!

My father was euphoric. "It's raining! I can't believe it! Rain!"

I was looking into the sky with tears in my eyes, like Jennifer Jones in *The Song of Bernadette.*

It was a miracle!

Quickly, we gathered up the food and dashed into the house. The big, cool house. The big, cool, wonderfully, fabulously, cold, freezing air-conditioned house.

"What a relief," my brother said, once we were all inside. "I couldn't take it anymore."

"I know," my mother said. "Leave it to Billy to have his birthday on the hottest day of the year."

Isn't she delightful?

An Oscar Fantasy

By the time our limousine pulled up to the Shrine Auditorium I was a nervous wreck, pale, shaking like a leaf.

"You look terrible," my mother said. "Have some sausage. You want some peppers and eggs? They're still hot."

She brought this whole shopping bag filled with food. I couldn't believe it.

"I'm too nervous to eat," I told her. "Look at all those photographers out there!"

"These things go on forever, and you know how you get," my mother said, pushing a sausage into my mouth. "Chew. Chew. Watch the grease. Go slow. Emilio, give me a napkin ..."

My father kept saying "Smile!" and pointing his stupid video camera at me. My brother Don was eating a hero sandwich; Joyce was sipping a Diet Coke. The fumes were starting to get to me.

"It smells like San Gennaro in here," I said, fanning my face. "Can somebody *please* open a window? I'm really starting to lose it."

"Don't forget to thank your aunt Irene," my mother told me. "And, if there's time, Joe and Marie next door. Here, take some bread; it'll calm your stomach. Did you find your speech yet?"

"No! It's in one of these pockets! I'm too nervous!"

"Don't worry about it," she said. "We'll all pray to St. Anthony. Everybody hold hands."

The next thing I knew, some kid in a red jacket was opening the door to the limo and a million flashbulbs exploded in my face.

Oh, God. What am I doing here?

We walked down a long red carpet, and Oprah asked about my tuxedo. I couldn't get the words out.

"Hi, Oprah," my mom said, pushing through the crowd. "I'm the mother. It's the J. C. Penney Doin' It Right tuxedo. I got one for each of them, $95, but my neighbor DeeDee works there, she's the manager of the better linens department in the Massapequa store, so we got the fifteen percent off. This is my husband Emilio, we're retired, and my son Donald, he's also very successful ... Donald, come here, say hello to Oprah ... Donald owns South Bay Collision in West Babylon ... Donald give Oprah a card ..."

My father, trying to get all of this on video, turns suddenly with the camera and hits Tom Cruise in the nose. Cruise falls to the ground. His wife, Nicole Kidman, is screaming. My brother spots Kidman and his jaw drops. Joyce threatens to go back to the limo.

Ten minutes later, we're through the door, looking for our seats. We wind up in the row behind Mira Sorvino and her father. My mother is telling all of us to go to the bathroom. I tell her I'm too nervous.

"Oh," she says, "and what are you going to do, wait until the cameras are rolling? The whole world has to know your business?"

Paul Sorvino turns around, sniffing. "Is that peppers and eggs?"

"Yes," my mother says. "You want some? Hold on."

"I haven't had that in years," Sorvino says.

"Well, then, it's about time," my mother tells him. "Look at you, you're skin and bones." She then pulls a loaf of Italian bread out of the shopping bag and holds it in front of him. He puts his index finger about four inches from the end. Then five inches. My mother moves it to eight. She then slices the bread, opens it up, and starts filling it with peppers and eggs. "I made it fresh this morning," she tells him. "You want a little cheese with that? Pecorino Romano."

John Travolta, walking by with his wife, Kelly Preston, winds up sitting across the aisle. The show is about to start. My brother is telling John how much he liked *Pulp Fiction* while my mother makes him a capocolla hero with fresh basil.

Handing Travolta the sandwich, she says, "I heard *Pulp.* I thought it was about tomatoes, but it had so much dirty talk I couldn't even look at it. Everything was *F.* They should have called it *Pulp F-Word.* You don't talk that way at home, do you?"

"No, Mrs. Ervolino," he said. "It was just for the movie. I'm a Scientologist."

"Well, it's good you have something to fall back on," she said. "There's a lot of money in science now, especially with the computers. How's your sandwich? You want some pepperoni? I went to the pork store this afternoon."

They had just announced Mira Sorvino's name in the supporting actress category. Paul was so excited he turned around to share the moment with us and got the pepperoni right in his eye. He yelped and then buried his face in his hands, just as the TV cameras focused on him.

"Oh my God!" I yelled. "Are you all right?"

Sorvino couldn't even talk, he was crying like a baby. Martin Scorsese rushed over to help him, but quickly looked up and started sniffing.

"Is that peppers and eggs?" he asked.

It was the longest night of my life.

Emilio at Seventy

Today is Emilio's seventieth birthday—an Ervolino milestone—so I figured it at least deserved a telephone interview. I also figured this would be a great way to talk to my father one on one, without his feeling uncomfortable about it. (Somehow, though, my mother screamed her way into the conversation. She's the one in italics.) A partial transcript:

Q: So what does it mean to turn seventy?

A: I don't know.

Q: Well, could you THINK about it? This is an interview. And a long-distance call.

A: *(laughing)* What do you want me to say?

Q: I don't know, Dad. I mean, come on: It must mean SOME-THING to you. Seventy's old.

A: I'm glad that I made seventy. Hopefully, I'll make eighty. But aside from that, I don't know what it means.

Q: Did you ever think you'd get this old?

A: Well, certainly, I'm thankful. And I'm thankful I have your mother here to keep me company.

Q: Even though she drives you crazy?

A: Yeah. But she's my companion for life. She kept me alive and I think I kept her alive. I think we did something good for each other. And the fact that we were there for each other kept us going. And that's it. She's making chicken sausage now. Do you want to talk to her?

Q: No! I'm interviewing you! What's your earliest memory?

A: Of what?

Q: Dad, who's on first? Your earliest memory of WHATEVER.

A: Well, unfortunately, I don't have too many memories. I don't remember seventeen or eighteen. Well, no, on my eighteenth birthday I went into the Navy for a year and a half. I was discharged in July of '46 and your mother was waiting on the stoop so she could latch on to me.

[A voice in the background]: *I was not!*

Q: Oh God. I can hear her screaming over the phone.

A: At that point we lived two doors away from each other. She moved in after I went into the service. I was on Johnston Island or Johnson Island. It's near Hawaii. Look on a map. Hawaii is over here and then there's a little dot over there, and that's the island I was on. And that's where I met John Welles, this guy who lived down the block, and he said she was waiting on the stoop for me.

That's a lie! I didn't even know he existed!

Anyway, he told me the Gangles—two old maids who made hats—sold their house to your mother's family. And he told me this young girl moved into the house.

Q: Did he say she was good-looking?

A: I don't remember him saying that.

Is he putting this in the paper?

Q: This is *so* cool! It's like *Back to the Future.* Then what happened?

A: There was also this other girl, Phyllis, waiting for me. She had a crush on me, too. So I was going to the ice cream parlor with Phyllis and I told her to ask Mommy, who was sitting on the stoop, to come with us. Then your mother and I left together, and the rest is history.

Q: Poor Phyllis. How could you do that to her?

A: About two to three weeks after I was home I asked your mother to marry me and she said I was crazy.

Q: Were you?

A: Probably. But we kept going out from 1946 to October 1948. That's when we got married. It was a football wedding. We had like a thousand people and I think it cost us $350. If I'm not mistaken we ran out of food and beer and had to ask them to order more food.

He's crazy! There was plenty of food! Don't listen to him!

Q: Why did they call it a football wedding?

A: Because it was all hero sandwiches and people would yell out, "Gimme a salami! Gimme a capocolla!" And you'd

throw them a sandwich. There were also big trays of cookies. They didn't have wedding cakes then. Cookies with little dots on them. What do you call them, those little dots?

Q: The Johnston Islands.

A: Sprinkles.

Q: And then you moved in with your mother?

A: Yeah, we lived with Grandma in two rooms in a four-room
railroad flat and the bathroom was in the hall. We stayed
there a few years and then we bought the house in
Rosedale (Queens) for $9,990, and we had to borrow the
$990 down payment.

Q: Why did you wait so long to have kids?

A: Because we made a list. I had to make $100 a week before
we had children, and I wanted a house and a Cadillac. We
got the house and the car pretty fast, but it took a few years
to get the $100. So you didn't come along for seven years.

Q: Well, thanks for fitting me in.

A: You're welcome. Then we waited another three years until
you were on your own for Donald. We wanted a girl, too,
but your mother was too old by then. She was thirty-one,
which is nothing today, but I guess in those days it was different.

Q: Are you satisfied with your life?

A: I think we're satisfied. I guess we wanted a little more, but
we're humble people. We had two nice children and a nice
home.

Q: How has retirement been?

A: Well, that's another story. It's all right. But we eat too much.
When you reach our age there's nothing else left to do. We
traveled a lot when we were younger and healthier, which
was good. Now traveling is an ordeal. We'd rather stay
home and eat.

Q: Do you have any advice for people?

A: About what?

Q: Well, you know: You're seventy. You're supposed to be wise.

A: Oh, I don't know. If you want to do something, do it. If you want to go somewhere, go. Save the United States for when you're older, overseas when you're younger. Take care of your wife.

Q: Do you feel old?

A: Not really. We look at people around our age and most of them are all gray haired, with canes or walkers, but we're still looking pretty young and feeling good. We have our problems but they're not life-threatening at this moment.

Q: Do you have a final word?

A: Be kind to one another, be there for one another, love one another, tolerate one another, I don't know … that's it. I'm waiting for them to take my car. Did I tell you about the car? There's a rotten egg smell in the Cadillac because of the catalytic converter. I finally got my recall and I'm waiting for them to pick it up.

Q: I love you, Dad.

A: Love you, too. Did I tell you about it? It smells just like rotten eggs.

Holy Days and Obligations

Her Passion Was a Dictator

We all go through our lives certain that we know our mothers like a book. Then one day we find out something we never knew before: that she once dated somebody famous, or that she was arrested for sneaking into a movie theater when she was twelve, or that before the operation her real name was Sidney.

This is sort of how I felt a few years ago when my mother told me that before becoming obsessed with Frank Sinatra, she had had a crush on—are you sitting down?—Benito Mussolini.

Hey, better I heard it from her than finding out about it on *A Current Affair* or *Rolonda*.

Besides, I think it's kind of hilarious. Frankie *and* Benito? Is it any wonder my poor father doesn't know whether he's coming or going?

Actually, if you do a little investigating, you'll find that there were more than a few similarities between these two famous men:

1. Frankie is Italian; so was Benito.
2. Frankie likes pizza with anchovies; so did Benito.

3. Frankie sang "I've Got the World on a String"; Benito declared war on Ethiopia, defied the sanctions of the League of Nations, joined the Berlin-Tokyo Axis, and sent troops to fight for Franco against the Republic of Spain.

Of course it goes without saying that my mother's affection for Benito predated World War II. Or, as she puts it, "before he hooked up with that Adolf Hitler." (Fickle, isn't she? For the record, her affection for Sinatra actually peaked during the mid-1940s, "before he hooked up with that Ava Gardner.")

All of this Mussolini business came out five or six years ago after an otherwise uneventful Sunday dinner. I asked my mother if she had been involved in any organizations when she was a kid growing up in Brooklyn, and she said, "No, not really. Just the Fascist Club. Could somebody pass the sugar?"

I almost gagged on my zabaglione. So did my father.

The Fascist Club? My mother was a *Fascist*?

I glanced toward my father and immediately knew what he was thinking: "The Fascist Club? My wife was a *Fascist*?"

Hmm ...

"Roses are red / Violets are blue / Happy Mother's Day / You Fascist, you."

"I was about nine years old," she said, "and everybody in the neighborhood belonged to it. We used to wear these cute hats and white shirts with black neckerchiefs and armbands. We'd march around with the Italian and American flags. It was like the Girl Scouts."

My mother was a Fascist?

I closed my eyes and conjured up this picture of her going door to door selling her little Fascist anisette cookies. Or getting together after school with her girlfriends to listen to records, comb their hair like Veronica Lake, and imagine what it'd be like to be married to some cute dictator somewhere.

BENITO: Honey, I'm home!

LOUISE: Oh, Benito ... it's been days.

BENITO: I'm sorry, *mi amore*. I was out conquering the
Balkans.

LOUISE: Really? Did you remember to pick up the cannolis?

"Before the war," my mother explained, "he was considered a great man who was very good to his people. My father even kept a statue of him in our bakery." (Can you imagine walking into a bakery and seeing something like that? *Benito says, "Try our Kaiser rolls!"*) "It was a beautiful statue. You could see it from the window. He was a pretty handsome man, you know."

Yeah, and I'm Rocky the Flying Squirrel.

"Anyway," she said, "then things got bad between Italy and the United States and my father did *something* with it. I don't know if he put it in a closet or got rid of it in the middle of the night."

(Now here's an image: World War II has just broken out, it's 2 A.M., and you're driving through Brooklyn with a statue of Mussolini, looking for a Dumpster …)

It was right around this time that my mother dropped Benito like a hot gnocchi and shifted her attention to Ol' Blue Eyes. It's an infatuation that continues to this day, although it was more or less derailed in 1948 when her family moved from the Williamsburg section of Brooklyn to East New York, and she met and married Emilio Ervolino, an ex-sailor who lived on her block and whose legs were just as skinny as Sinatra's. Now that I think about it, there were other similiarities as well:

1. Frankie is Italian; so is Emilio.
2. Frankie likes his calamari with medium-hot sauce; so does Emilio.
3. Frankie sang "Strangers in the Night"; Emilio married the girl next door and then found out, forty-one years later, that she had been a Fascist and had had a crush on Mussolini.

"Roses are red/Violets are blue/Happy Mother's Day, whoever you are/Doobie-doobie-do."

Cholesterol Ergo Sum

Back in the glorious, prewomen's lib, precholesterol days of my youth, when Italian women were perfectly content to stay home and cook twenty-four hours a day, the week before Easter was particularly busy. In fact, I think the only time my mother walked away from her rolling pin was to answer the telephone.

"Hello? Hi. Yeah. I'm making my pies. You making your pies? How are your pies coming? Did you finish your pies yet? Well, I gotta get back to my pies."

And I'm not talking apple pies, blueberry pies, or any of those other gooey sticky-bun, Aunt Bee-rhubarb things that they make a fuss over in Mayberry.

I'm talking *manly* pies.

Macaroni pies.

Meat pies.

Ricotta pies.

Pies that can kill you.

The ricotta, or "sweet" pie, similar in texture to an American cheesecake, is made with ricotta cheese, some sweet stuff, and about seventy eggs.

The macaroni pie, dense and chewy, is made out of broken-up spaghetti, more cheese, and about four hundred eggs.

And the meat pie—a quiche the size of Albania—is made with meat (sopressata, prosciutto, etc.), more cheese, seventeen thousand eggs, and has to be removed from the oven on a forklift.

Should it slip at any point, it will rip through floors, earth, and granite.

JANE FONDA: The China syndrome?
JACK LEMMON: Yes, that's possible.

Now, unless you're a Sumo wrestler, you don't want to eat too much of this stuff since it tends to puff up your middle. It also seeks out all the salt, pepper, and lemon juice in your bloodstream and turns your arteries into hollandaise.

On the other hand, you have to remember that for centuries Italians used these pies to break their strict Good Friday fasts—another tradition my family took very seriously.

Our meager Good Friday dinner was usually limited to a little antipasto with some fresh roasted peppers and a couple of wedges of imported provolone, followed by a few bowls of spaghetti with clam sauce and maybe ten or twenty pounds of shrimps. The small ones.

And that was *it.*

More or less.

I can still remember my brother pleading for a hot dog, and my mother screaming, "Do you want God to hear you? We're suffering! Pass the lobster tails!"

When Jews fast during their High Holy Days, they usually look ashen and frail for days.

Italians detonate.

In fact, it's not uncommon in the week after Easter to walk down the street and see all these little Italian men spinning through the air and exploding.

Oh, the humanity.

Perhaps this is why, in recent years, so many Italian women have stopped making their Easter pies. Ever since all this cholesterol business started, they can't pick up a carton of eggs without feeling like criminals.

Lizzie Borden took some yolks and gave her family forty strokes.

Guilt out of the way, there is also the work to consider. An Italian Easter pie isn't exactly a piece of cake. And it isn't something you can start on Monday and finish four days later when the swelling in your ankles goes down.

An Italian Easter pie is a commitment.

After shopping for the ingredients, you have to start sifting all that flour, and chopping all those meats, and blending all those cheeses, and cooking all that spaghetti, and cracking open hundreds of thousands of eggs.

You also have to figure out on what sort of scale you're going to do all of this since, by Holy Thursday, all of your relatives who *don't* bake for Easter start sniffing around like the pie-sucking rodents they are.

None of this, I'm proud to say, has ever deterred my mother. Until last Tuesday. That's when she called me on the telephone and started talking in her I'm-too-sick-to-go-to-school voice.

"I was just won-der-ing," she said, creaking like an old sewing machine. "Would you mind if I didn't make the pies this year?"

"I don't know what you're talking about," I said. "Who is this? I think you have the wrong number."

"No, this is serious," she said. "I don't think I should make the pies this year. Your father has a heart condition."

"Well, that's true," I said, trying to be as diplomatic as possible. "On the other hand, the pies are a tradition he always enjoyed. I hardly think it's fair to deprive him of the pleasure of watching us eat them."

"Your brother can't eat them, either," she said. "His allergies have gotten so bad in the last few months. He has cold cuts and he gets so dizzy he can't stand up."

"Of course he has allergies! He spent the first seventeen years of his life eating nothing but hot dogs! But what about the rest of us? Can't you just make a small pie? Just a baby one? A really teeny-tiny, itsy-bitsy …"

"A small pie is just as much trouble as a big one," she insisted.

"Well, can't you make them and not tell anybody?"

"No, I tried that last year. As soon as your father sees ten dozen eggs in the refrigerator he gets suspicious. Besides, it's so much work …"

Well, OK! Fine! Don't make the pies! Who cares? Let's just eat a salad! Let's just eat nuts and berries! Let's all live to be 100!

Hey, there are those cranky, old Ervolinos sitting in the corner, eating their bean sprouts. Don't they look happy?

Hmm …

Now what?

Most rotten, miserable, selfish kids, when they really, really want something, will moan, groan, beg, plead, whine, and scream.

Don't you hate that?

I don't.

I moaned, groaned, begged, pleaded, whined, and screamed for fifteen minutes. I knew she'd come around eventually.

"Well, I suppose your father *could* have a little slice," she said. "It's only once a year ..."

"It is. It is."

"And I guess your brother *could* pick out the prosciutto ..."

"He could. He could."

"But then ... promise me you'll take the rest home."

Take the *rest* home?

I started jumping and up and down: "I promise! Yes! Deal! Bingo! I love you, Mommy, dearest!"

Five minutes later it hit me: a whole meat pie for myself? The woman's trying to kill me.

Geeks Bearing Gifts

When no one tells you what they want for Christmas, they deserve whatever stupid thing you give them.

A couple of years ago out of sheer desperation, I wandered into this store called the Sharper Image and bought a Christmas present for my cousin Caroline, who was fifteen.

The gift was a handheld alarm—ostensibly the loudest handheld alarm ever made—and I thought it would come in handy on those dark, dreary nights when Caroline was walking home from her baby-sitting job.

All you have to do, the salesman explained to me, is hit two or three buttons on the side of this thing—bip, bip, bip—and all hell would break loose: the loudest, shrillest, screeching-est noise you've ever heard in your life—ten times louder than your average car alarm.

Then, after your assailant runs off screaming with blood pouring out his ears, you hit a few other buttons—bip, bip, bip—and the alarm disengages.

An odd Christmas gift? Sure. But part of me thought it was a good idea. I mean, there had been some problems in Caroline's neighborhood, and she didn't have a car, and she couldn't always get a ride home from my aunt.

So why not?

Besides, I thought to myself, this was one of those pièce de résistance presents. You know: The person opens it up toward the end of the night on Christmas Eve, it does something really unusual, and the next day, everybody's still talking about it.

And sure enough, when she opened the box on Christmas Eve, everybody was oohing and aahing.

Look at that! What is it? How does it work?

"Allow me," I said, grinning like a total geek. (How does that old saying go: Beware of geeks bearing gifts?) I then turned on the alarm and—bip, bip, bip, bip, bip, bip, bip, bip—couldn't shut it off to save my life.

I bipped. I bip-bipped. I bip-bip-bipped.

Silent night, it wasn't.

This thing was screeching, howling, piercing eardrums, shattering windows, people were holding their ears, my aunt and my mother ran screaming from the room, and I couldn't shut it off until one of my cousins finally grabbed it from my hand and ripped the batteries out.

"Good God," my father yelled.

My aunt Irene looked at me as if I'd just given her daughter a nuclear missile.

The next day everybody was still talking about it.

I have no idea what happened to the alarm—no one ever mentioned it again. But that little purchase did put me on the Sharper Image mailing list, which means that every month I get this catalog filled with all sorts of similar, useless, high-tech lunacy.

I sat down with the store's most recent catalog last week, when my parents, the esteemed Emilio and Louise, *still* wouldn't tell me what they wanted for Christmas.

They do this every year: I tell them *exactly* what I want; they tell me, "We have everything we need."

Well, OK, I guess it's time to teach them a lesson. So, for the couple who has everything, I've finally narrowed it down to:

1. A $35 talking picture frame. The frame has a recording device built in so you can record the voice of the person in the picture and play it back whenever the mood strikes. As the catalog explains, "Nothing is as comforting as the voice of a loved one." ("Emilio, mow the lawn! Emilio, mow the lawn!") Tempting.
2. A $50 golf club that is clear, hollow, and holds four cigars. "Imagine the reaction of your golfing buddies when you pull the new Cigar Wedge from your bag," the catalog says. (Before they fall to the floor laughing or after?) My father doesn't play golf, smoke cigars, or have any buddies. Sounds perfect to me.
3. The $89.95 Turbo Auto Drive Tie Rack is a battery-operated turbo-charged rotating tie rack that allows you to "review" up to seventy-two ties in less than ten seconds. I know my father

would get his finger stuck in this thing and spin around the closet for days until my mother realized he was missing.

4. An "awesome" $280, twenty-seven-inch-high lava lamp. I love this one. Perfect for those long winter nights when Emilio and Louise kick back, drop acid, and listen to the *Forrest Gump* soundtrack.

5. A $795 limited edition twenty-six-inch sculpture of Yoda, the gnomish Jedi Master with the wrinkled face and big ears from *The Empire Strikes Back*. This is a guaranteed collectors item, and my mother loves collectibles. On the other hand, I can't imagine any woman wanting to live with two twenty-six-inch-tall, wrinkled, big-eared gnomes. But I'm thinking about it, anyway.

6. A $129.95 Radar Watchdog with Intruder Alarm. This is a ten-inch alarm device with a radar detector that can sense motion through walls and doors and then—I *love* this part—it starts barking. And when the intruder gets closer, the barking gets louder. And when the intruder takes out the batteries, it bites him. (No, only kidding. But I'm sure my mother would bite him. Same difference.)

7. A $350 Linear Wet/Dry Shaver. Egads: "Through electromagnetic repulsion and attraction, the blades on this revolutionary Panasonic shaver move at an incredible 12,000 strokes per minute." Can you imagine this? In just under three seconds you could shave your face, legs, underarms, ears, nose, and throat, trim wallpaper, cut cookie dough, shorten pants, and God knows what else ...

"Emilio, mow the lawn! Emilio, mow the lawn!"

Can you imagine a little Italian man being dragged through the grass by an out-of-control electromagnetic shaver?

I can.

The New Little Village

I am returning to Long Island today for—somebody get me a Valium—the official unveiling of the New Little Village.

By all reports, the New Little Village is a vast improvement over the Old Little Village, an Ervolino holiday tradition that dates all the way back to 1991.

Time flies, doesn't it?

The Old Little Village was my father's idea. It started with four little plastic houses lovingly arranged under my parents' stately plastic Christmas tree.

Yuletide visitors would invariably stop by to see the stately plastic Christmas tree, look down at the four little plastic houses, and say, "Well, aren't they cute?"

My father, Emilio, the proud papa of the Old Little Village, would invariably nod his head, rub his fat little belly, and say, "I'm thinking of doing even more next year."

And so he did.

The following Christmas, Emilio gave birth to another set of quadruplets. His four little plastic houses now had two more little plastic houses to play with, along with a little plastic church and a little plastic town hall, all nestled in a magical bed of cotton.

Yuletide visitors would invariably stop by, look down at the newly expanded Old Little Village, and say, "Why, it's even cuter than last year!"

For those of you with any sort of psychological background, this is called positive reinforcement. A valuable tool in corporate management and potty training, it is not something to be tossed around lightly when dealing with senior citizens who have too much time on their hands.

Had I been thinking straight that second year, I would have looked at the newly expanded Old Little Village, told my father, "Bad, bad ..." and zapped him with a cattle prod.

But I didn't.

By 1993, my mother had joined the act and—playing Barnum to his Bailey, Leona to his Harry, A to his T&T—she turned Emilio's cute plastic cottages into a cottage industry.

Louise Does Levittown.

In the sweeping shadow of my mother's bold architectural vision, the Little Village—once confined to a tiny area to the left of the stately plastic Christmas tree—suddenly consumed half the living room.

There were more houses! More churches! *Plus:* mountains, rivers, roads, electric streetlights, skating rinks, carolers, animals, and so much cotton that boll weevils were clawing at the living-room windows at all hours of the day and night.

By 1994, the Little Village had gotten big enough to be given—are you sitting down?—its *own* Little Village.

The Little Village's Little Village was a group of teeny-tiny little plastic houses that ran across the windowsill and looked down on the Bigger Little Village.

"That," my mother said of the new addition, "is another Little Village ... in the distance."

"What a good idea," I said, smiling politely.

By this point, the 1993 mountains had been replaced with what my father referred to as "more realistic-looking" mountains, and the cotton snow had been replaced with "more realistic-looking" snow.

"We're trying to get real," he told me.

Keep trying, Dad.

Simultaneously, the Little Village's little plastic animal population grew to include dogs, reindeers, cows, giraffes ...

"Exactly what country is this Little Village in?" I asked.

The 1994 village lasted through 1995 with nary a spill nor scrape—a model for Little Villages everywhere. But then, over this past summer, something happened. A collectibles store on Long Island announced it was going out of business and proceeded to put together a Little Village blowout.

Sometime in July, my mother called and said, "You're not going to believe what your crazy father and I just did ..."

I took a deep breath. "He didn't put on his Batman costume and tie you to the headboard again, did he?"

"No, no, no," she told me. What she and my crazy father had done was spend $3,000 on a New Little Village.

"You did … *what?*"

"Oh, wait'll you see it," she told me. "It's all department 56!"

"What the hell is department 56?"

"It's a collectible," she replied.

Collectibles used to be cheap, old things that people discovered were worth money after they bought them for nothing at garage sales. Today, they are expensive new things sold in specialty stores, which come in boxes that say "This is a collectible." You hold on to them for a while because they're so valuable, but no one wants to buy them from you, so you wind up selling them for nothing at garage sales.

"Anyway," she told me, "your father and I had a long talk and we have decided to divide up the old Little Village. We're giving half of it to Aunt Irene and the other half to cousin Anthony and Wendy, so they can get started."

All of this sounded vaguely like that scene in *The Godfather, Part II,* when Hyman Roth announced he was divvying up his casino interests between the Corleone family, Bruno Tattaglia, and the Pennino Brothers.

"But don't worry," she told me. "Someday, you will split the New Little Village with your brother, Donald. Providing you're good, of course … ha-ha-ha."

"I see."

For those of you with any sort of psychological background, this is called negative reinforcement.

Nightmare Before Christmas

Last year, for some odd reason, I thought it might be nice to invite a woman I knew to my parents' house for Christmas Eve. I thought it might be fun for a non-Italian to see how an Italian family celebrates the holidays. I thought she and my mother would hit it off like partridges and pear trees.

So I was wrong. So sue me.

When I extended the invitation to Karen, she was enthusiastic. "Sounds fine to me," she said. And when I mentioned to my mother that I was bringing a friend, she was thrilled. "Sounds fine to me," she said. So it sounded fine to them and it sounded fine to me, and everything sounded hunky-dory with everybody. What more could I want?

It should be pointed out that in Italian households, Christmas Eve is the social event of the season—an Italian woman's reason for living. She cleans. She cooks. She bakes. She orchestrates every minute of the evening.

I should also point out that Karen is the kind of woman Italian men are irresistibly drawn to. She doesn't cook. She doesn't bake. And she makes Dolly Parton look flat-chested. I brought her anyway.

The Arrival

Karen and I walk in at about 7 P.M. and putter around for half an hour waiting for the other guests to show up. During that time my mother grills Karen like a cheeseburger and cagily determines that she and Karen have nothing in common. My father makes the same determination. He pulls me aside, slaps his forehead, and says, "Good God! She makes Dolly Parton look flat-chested!"

At 7:30 the doorbell rings and in marches Uncle Ziti and Aunt Mafalda, with gifts, children, pastries, the whole nine yards. We sit around the dining-room table and my mother brings out two platters of antipasto: symmetrically arranged salads containing lettuce, roasted peppers, black olives, salami, provolone, and anchovies.

When I offer to make Karen's plate, she says, "Thank you. Just don't give me any of those things, OK?" She's pointing to the anchovies.

"You don't like anchovies?" I ask.

"I don't like fish," she tells me while thirty-five other varieties of the little devils are baking, broiling, and simmering in the next room.

Within seconds, my jaw drops, my mother's jaw drops, and my aunt Mafalda makes the sign of the cross. My brother asks Karen what her family eats on Christmas Eve and she says, "Knockwurst." My father, who is still staring in a daze at Karen's chest, suddenly murmurs, "Knockers?" My mother kicks his leg so hard he gets a blood clot. None of this is turning out the way I'd hoped.

Second Course

As the spaghetti with crab sauce makes its way to the table, Karen declines the sauce and offers to make her own, with butter and ketchup.

"No problem," my mother says cheerfully, flying into the kitchen like the monster in *Alien*. I remove my Merry Christmas napkin from my lap and walk in after her.

"I don't want to start any trouble," my mother says calmly, clutching the ketchup bottle in her hand, "but if she pours this on my pasta, I'm going to throw acid in her face."

I remind her it's Christmas and she should just let the woman eat what she wants.

"Tell me the truth," she says, gritting her teeth, "are you serious with this tramp?"

I say she's not a tramp and we're just friends.

"Fine," she says, walking back toward the dining room. "Because I'm telling you right now: If you marry her, she'll poison you."

Clearing the Table

All the women at the table get up to clear away the spaghetti dishes, bowls, platters, and glasses, except for Karen, who lights a cigarette. Eventually, she gets up and brings a dirty fork into the kitchen.

"That was so nice of you, dear," my mother says.

"No problem," Karen says. As she walks back into the dining room, a steak knife comes flying over her head and embeds itself in the wall.

From the kitchen, my mother says, "Oops!"

When the fish finally comes out, platters and platters of it, Karen decides to try the scungilli, which she describes as "slimy, like worms."

My mother winces, bites her hand, and begins pounding her chest. My aunt Mafalda does likewise. Karen, thinking this is something all Italian women do on Christmas Eve, starts to pound her chest, too. And my father's mouth opens so wide that his dentures fall out.

Espresso, Dessert

The pot of espresso finally comes to the table with Sambuca and small curls of lemon peel. When Karen pours herself a cup and asks for milk, my mother finally cracks, picking up a cannoli and slapping Karen across the face with it. Karen, believing this is something all Italian women do on Christmas Eve, picks up a cannoli and slaps my mother with it.

"Hey, this is fun," Karen says.

Yeah, right. Merry Christmas, everybody.

Giving Thanks Fast

The Fab Four Ervolinos reunited on Thanksgiving Day for turkey, etc., minus the bevy of aunts, uncles, cousins, boyfriends, girlfriends, and assorted others who usually crowd around the table and give us something to talk about.

My brother's girlfriend Joyce had the flu, and none of my friends wanted to make the trip with me from New Jersey to Long Island (thirty-seven hours, bumper to bumper). My aunt Irene was spending the day with her kids and her brand-new grandson. And the rest of the herd was previously engaged.

Hmm …

Cooking for fewer than forty people has always made my mother doubt her worth as an Italian woman. Still, there seemed something special about its being just the four of us.

Imagine: John, Paul, George, and Emilio, together again for the first time since they decided to let it be in 1969.

We might have even sung "Free as a Bird" had there not been a dead stuffed one in the middle of the table.

After some stimulating small talk ("Could somebody pass the salt?") we dug into a formidable groaning board of turkey, mashed potatoes, sweet potatoes, corn fritters, creamed spinach, creamed onions, mushrooms, asparagus, stuffing, corn bread, pumpernickel, and hot, fluffy biscuits.

Ten minutes later, we were done, which threw my mother into a postpartum depression unrivaled in the annals of modern psychiatry.

First, she stood up and started crying.

Then she started rubbing her hands on her face.

Don't you hate it when mothers get all soggy and miserable? Then just to break up the monotony, she screamed.

Loud.

"I spent four days preparing this meal!"

Don't you hate it when mothers get all loud and crazy?

Instinctively, the Daddy Bear and the two Baby Bears grabbed something off the nearest platter and quickly stuffed it down their throats, paying no attention to whether it was too hot, too cold, too big, too small, too hard, or too fluffy.

"Mmm ..." I said, chewing ferociously. "Mmm! Mmm!"

"Four days!"

Oy.

"Mmm!"

"Mmm!"

"Mmm!"

Of course, there were only so many times we could get away with that little ploy. We were so exhausted and full of food—tripping on tryptophan—that we could barely lift our arms.

The amount we had consumed, however, clearly was not the point. My mother looked around, saw the dining room cluttered with plates, the kitchen sink littered with pots, and burst into tears.

"How could you eat all that food in ten minutes?" she wailed.

It was obvious that we'd sunk her gravy boat, and we all felt awful about it. Although, for the record, the Ervolinos have always been fast eaters. In fact, in Italian, "Ervolino" means "What happened to all that salami I bought yesterday?"

No matter. In her postturkey delirium she was convinced that our finishing dinner in ten minutes was a reflection on us as a family—that we didn't love each other anymore.

"Oh, that's ridiculous," I told her, trying to be as diplomatic as possible. "I still love you, Daddy, and Ronald very much."

MOM:	His name is Donald!
ME:	Ronald, Donald ... whatever ...
MOM:	*Waahhh ...*
DAD:	Besides, we've always been fast eaters.
DON:	That's right. We eat fast, because your food is *so good.*
MOM:	(*sniffling*): Really? I thought it meant we weren't close anymore.
ME:	Of course we're close. We just ate a little faster today because there was no one here to talk to.
MOM:	*Waahhh ...*

ME: What I mean is, there was no one here we had anything
       new to say to.
MOM: *Waahhh ...*
ME: What I mean is ...
DAD: Billy, shut up.

An hour or so later, my still-tense mother made coffee and set the
table with a spread of pies and pastries. This time we were prepared,
and more sensitive to her needs, although I chewed one cannoli for
so long, my jaw started aching.

DON: What do you have in your mouth?
ME: (confused): I don't know ... I can't remember ...

We spent the rest of the night curled up in front of the TVs—my
mother watching a movie in her bedroom, my father watching a ball
game in the living room, and my brother and me, in the den, watching the final installment of The Beatles' reunion.

It didn't exactly bring us closer together, but it gave us some interesting things to talk about when we met each other in the hall during commercials.

The Power Washer

A few days before Father's Day I discovered that I was chipping in with my brother on a special gift for dear old Dad.

"I got him something he really wanted," Don insisted. "It cost $200. You can go 50–50 with me."

"Fine with me," I said, although $100 each for a Father's Day gift seemed a bit much. "So … uh … what are we giving him?"

"He's gonna love it!" my brother insisted. "I bought him … the *Power Washer!*"

"Oh. What's that?"

"Haven't you seen it? It's like this really, really powerful hose. It cleans everything. It's called … the *Power Washer.*"

I like my brother but he can be a little weird sometimes.

"I don't understand," I said. "You spent $200? For a hose?"

"It's not a hose," he said. "It's … the *Power Washer!* He's gonna love it!"

Probably.

Some people as they get older collect stamps, or coins, or ceramic elephants. My father collects high-tech gardening equipment—the sort of insane, high-power gadgets that Arnold Schwarzenegger and Bruce Willis do *their* gardening with.

Rake Hard with a Vengeance.

Four years ago, he insisted on having one of those strap-on-your-back leaf blowers that professional landscapers use. Could somebody please tell me why a ninety-five-pound Italian man with no yard to speak of needs a strap-on-your-back leaf blower?

And, of course, the second he strapped it on his back and turned it on, he blew right up a tree. My mother spent three quarters of an hour trying to pull him down with that big wooden spaghetti fork she keeps hanging in the kitchen.

Two years ago, he had to have a motorized rototiller. And then there was the Grasshopper, a four-wheel contraption he insisted on buying so he could weed his garden without having to bend over.

As far as I'm concerned, if you're too old to bend over, you're too old to use anything that has pointy edges, runs on gasoline, or says "Caution!" on the box.

He didn't need any more of these things. But, hey, it was Father's Day, and my brother had already bought it, so why not make the old guy happy, right?

Well, sure enough, when he unwrapped the package, his eyes just about bulged out of his head. "I can't believe it!" he said. "It's ... the *Power Washer*. It's just what I wanted! Thanks kids!"

"You're welcome," I told him. "Use it in good health."

That *is* what you're supposed to say when you give someone a new hose, isn't it?

My mother was all smiles until she started reading all the warnings on the carton. "Wait a minute," she said, "what *is* this thing?"

According to the box, the Power Washer cleans cedar shingles, driveways, asphalt, and "shoots a powerful blast of water up to 600 feet!"

For what possible reason?

My mother, who had been hearing him talk about this thing for weeks, suddenly looked nervous. "You said you'd be able to use this thing to clean the windows on the house."

"It'll do that easy," my father promised. "All you have to do is adjust the power."

"Oh."

I'm telling you right now, I know *exactly* what's going to happen: My mother will be sitting in the living room reading one of her Barbara Cartland novels ... she'll look up because she hears "a little noise" ... and two thousand gallons of water will come surging through the windows, like *The Poseidon Adventure*.

She'll start swimming toward the front door—with chandeliers, Hummels, and baby pictures floating all around her—and, I'm telling you, it's gonna be a mess.

Dad, of course, had to try the thing out immediately. So, as the rest of us set up the dining-room table for coffee and cake, he went out to the yard and hooked the thing up.

"Should I go out and help him?" I asked my mother.

"No, let him play," she said.

The next thing I knew, this hose was flying all around the yard like a sea serpent with my father hanging on to it for dear life, and there was water shooting everywhere you looked, breaking things, scaring birds, knocking down trees.

"I told you he'd like it," my brother said.

When he's right, he's right.

The Christmas List

By the third week in November I was already getting threatening phone calls from my mother. "Make up a Christmas list—*or else!*"

All you have to do is say the word "holiday" to an Italian woman and she turns into Doctor Doom.

"I don't want any excuses," she told me. "Write it all out, be specific, and mail it to me, or read it to me over the phone. I want to start my shopping early this year. I'm really in the mood. Your father and I are watching *The Bishop's Wife. Emilio! It's Billy on the phone! I told him to make out his list!* Your father says hello."

Doctor Doom loves Loretta Young movies. Also *Miracle on 34th Street,* which she always refers to as *Miracle on 42nd Street.*

"It says in the *TV Guide* that *Miracle on 42nd Street* is on Thursday, but they don't tell you which version it is."

"It's probably the one on 34th Street."

I forgot to make the list up in time to bring it there for Thanksgiving but had it completed by the following Sunday, the night before I was leaving for Florida. I called her a little after 11 P.M. She was already in bed.

"I'm sorry I'm calling so late," I said, "but I'm catching a plane in the morning. It's leaving at ten thirty, which means I have to be at the airport by nine thirty, which means I have to leave the house by eight thirty, which means I have to get to bed and wake up in about fifteen minutes. So do you want my list or not?"

"Yes. Let me get a pen. Emilio, do you have a pen? Emilio? *Emilio?*" Long pause.

"He *is* breathing, isn't he?"

"He's sleeping. Hold on."

Five minutes later I gave her the list, making clear to her that I didn't expect everything that was on it; I just wanted her to have a choice.

"I'd like a plain white dress shirt," I told her, "at least eighty percent cotton, no buttons on the pockets; a hooded sweatshirt, large; a pair of Levi 501s, that's the button-fly, regular ones, none of that acid-washed junk; white cotton sweat socks; and *please* no underwear. You get them for me every year and I have six hundred pairs.

"If I have to open another $4 worth of foil and ribbons and find $3 worth of shorts inside, I'm throwing them out the window.

"I have no Beatles CDs and I'd like to replace most of my albums, so I'll take any of them, but especially the *White Album, Revolver, Meet The Beatles,* and *Sgt. Pepper's.* On video, I'd like *The Godfather* parts one and two. I like two better than one, but my real preference is *The Godfather Saga,* which is parts one and two in chronological order— the version they showed on TV. I don't want part three unless it comes together with the other ones in a package and it's cheaper that way.

"I'd also like a bible. It doesn't have to be a fancy one; just something I can have in the house and use as a reference if I need it. And that's that. If anybody wants to get me something expensive, I wouldn't mind an espresso machine or a camcorder; just let me know if someone is buying one or the other for me so I don't get them something cheap and feel embarrassed.... Are you getting all of this?"

"Wait a second," she said. "Meatballs and Dr. Pepper?"

"Ma, what are you *talking* about?"

I think I called her just as her Xanax was kicking in.

One week later, I returned from Florida, returned the phone call, and returned the favor. "Tell me what you want for Christmas," I said. "I want a list. Now. Speak."

"We don't need anything," she said—the same thing she says every year. "Save your money. Buy something for yourself. We have everything we need. Christmas is for children. We don't ..."

"Ma, I'm in no mood for this, so cut the crap and give me a list."

"We'll call you back," she said.

Two hours later, the phone rang. Dad. He told me he wanted a parka, the warmer the better, any color, three-quarter length. "Just make sure it covers my ass," he said. "It gets cold in the winter."

"The weather or your ass?"

At least this was something practical.

With him out of the way, Doctor Doom got on the horn. "You can get me a flannel nightgown, any color, as long as it has a high collar because I have a skinny neck like Audrey Hepburn. And slippers, but they have to have a heel. Not a high heel, I'll break my neck, but a wedgie heel. Any color. My robe is yellow so it'll go with anything. And I could really use a pair of long johns. Large."

Try to imagine Audrey Hepburn's neck on Ernest Borgnine's thighs.

"You really want long johns?"

"Yeah. Every morning I walk a mile with Marie from next door. We go around the corner to the school and walk around the track. And my behind gets cold."

That's my parents: warm hearts, cool tushies.

After forty-six years they finally have something in common.

Home Is Where ...

The Prince Paints

(SYNOPSIS: Unable to find a painter, cabinetmaker, itinerant handyman, or traveling minstrel to paint his kitchen cabinets, Prince William decides to do the job himself and journeys to exotic, far-off Paramus to seek the sage advice of some jolly, big-bellied know-it-all at Home Depot.)

"Greetings," Prince William says to the duke of the toilet bowl department, just before collapsing on the counter.

"Forsooth," says the duke from his porcelain throne, "thou looketh flushed."

"Indeed," notes Prince William. "For I have cometh many miles to discuss the painting of cabinetry. Would thou be so kind as to direct me to the thane of Latex Enamel?"

The duke points to his left and wishes the prince godspeed. The prince thanks him and proceeds on foot, over hill and dale: past the lighting department, the wiring department, the aluminum siding department, the screwdriver department, the tool belt department, and the big, loud, scary, buzzing things department.

"Greetings," Prince William says to the earl of the earl burner department, gasping for breath. "Ppp … ppp … paint?"

The earl points to his left and wishes the prince godspeed. The prince punches him in the nose.

Shortly before dusk, the prince arrives at the paint department, where he meets the thane of Latex Enamel, a roguish rascal with a mischievous glint in his eye. (At least the prince *thought* it was a mischievous glint. Actually, it was a stray drop of Misty Mandarin Coral 8392, which is specially formulated for precise computer color matching.)

"I bring thee good tidings," says the prince. "And this ugly drawer."

The prince opens a plastic bag and pulls out an ugly drawer that he cleverly took from his kitchen so that the thane might athertane ... uh ... *ascertain* the most effective course of action.

"I have been told this is a fruitless task," Prince William says, "but I have come to seek your guidance as to whether or not it is possible to paint my cabinetry white. I have discussed this very same possibility with—"

Before the prince can finish, the thane hands him a gallon of primer-sealer, two sponge brushes, a roll of masking tape, and a clear plastic drop cloth.

He then says, "We have Bone White, Navajo White, China White, Spanish White, Antique White, Absolute White, Ultra-Pure White, White Linen, White Dove, Atrium White, Pearl White, Pelican White, Eggshell White, Cameo White, White Coffee, Imperial White, White Chiffon, Country White, Cottage White, Perry White, Betty White, and Barry ("Can't Get Enough of Your Love, Babe") White."

The prince shrugs his small but noble shoulders and says, "Uh ... Cottage White?"

"OK," says the thane. "One coat primer, wait an hour, two coats white, and you're done."

The prince is dumbstruck. "That's it?" he asks.

The thane nods and smiles. "Nothing to it," he says.

A half an hour later, back at the castle, the prince looks at his clock and does some calculations: One coat primer, wait an hour, two coats white, and you're done.

Hmm ...

It is 7:30. The prince figures he will be done by 10:30. The prince is an idiot.

At 8:10, still trying to figure out how to unwrap the drop cloth, the prince is growing testy.

At 9:50, as he continues to wrap masking tape along the surface of everything that isn't a kitchen cabinet, the prince is growing weary.

At 10:10, as the prince finally begins to apply the primer, his telephone rings.

At 10:30, still on the telephone, the prince realizes he has been tracking primer through his kitchen, dining room, and living room. He looks at the bottom of his princely sock, sees a large princely spot, and yells, "There is treachery afoot!"

At 11:45, the prince begins to apply the primer in earnest and by 1 A.M. begins to apply the first coat of Cottage White with the finesse of an *artiste*.

He continues this until about 2 A.M. when, overcome by fumes, he slips into the sink, falls backward onto the floor, and hits his head on a pine serving cart, which was unpainted until the prince fell on it.

Admitting that he is but a humble peasant in this baffling milieu of drawers and doors, arts and crafts, the *artiste*—formerly known as prince—finishes the first coat, pops the covers back on his cans, takes a shower, and hits the sack.

All in all, he has had a crappy night.

Clean and Single

A new singles guide—as if another one is going to make any differ-ence—suggests that when inviting a date to your home for the first time, it's a good idea to *really* clean the place up beforehand—in order to make, in the author's words, "the best possible impression."

Gee, I wish I'd thought of that.

I did notice, however, that there was no mention of what to do with your apartment on the third date. Or the fifth. Or the twelfth. Which got me to thinking:

My friend Chuck, who became "suddenly single" a few months ago, is suddenly dating again. His apartment is spotless.

My friend Steve is in a "committed" relationship. His apartment looks like something out of that movie *Twister*.

In fact, when I was over there last week, a cow blew out of a closet door, careened across the living room, and crashed through a picture window.

When I was talking to my friend Danny on the telephone a cou-ple of days later, he complained that his apartment was a "borderline" disaster area.

"Dating anyone in particular?" I asked.

"Actually, I have been," he told me. "And it's getting serious."

Hmm …

Hey, I'll be the first to admit how thrilled I am when someone comes to my apartment for the first time and says, "Your place is so clean! Let's make love!"

But as these relationships become more familiar, things have a way of changing for the worst. I've seen it. I've been there. I took notes.

Checklist: First Date

1. Tidy up living room. Vacuum rug. Stack old newspapers in neat four-foot piles. Dust lamp shades. Straighten pictures. Wipe tabletops. Remove Doritos, Tostitos, and all other -itos from

between sofa cushions. Fluff pillows. Take a few deep, fortifying breaths. Feels great, doesn't it? Move on.

2. Tidy up bedroom. Vacuum rug. Stack old newspapers in neat four-foot piles. Dust lamp shades. Collect socks, underwear, shirts, and pants from floor. Determine which socks, underwear, shirts, and pants belong in the bureau and which ones belong in the laundry bag. Remove Doritos, Tostitos, and all other -itos from between pillows. Make bed. Proudly wipe the sweat from your brow. Hey, this is better than a workout! Move on.

3. Tidy up kitchen. Sweep floor. Mop floor. Wash enormous pile of dishes. Dry enormous pile of dishes. Hey, this isn't so bad! Put enormous pile of dishes away. Clean countertops. Fill colorful bowls with Doritos, Tostitos and all other -itos. Lean against table until your head stops pounding. Move on.

4. Tidy up bathroom. Scrub tub, sink, and floor. Scrub toilet, toilet tank, bottom of toilet, sides of toilet, toilet rim, under toilet rim, top of lid, bottom of lid—who designed this stupid thing anyway?—and toilet seat. Put out clean towels. Replace assorted soap chips with a whole new bar. Arrange Mighty Morphin Power Ranger bubble bath action figures at attractive angles. Give waterbugs $10 to go to the movies. Hyperventilate.

Checklist: Third Date

1. Tidy up living room. Vacuum rug. Push old newspapers into a corner. Blow dust off lamp shades. Fluff pillows. Catch your breath. No point in going crazy.

2. Tidy up bedroom. Quickly pick a few things off the rug with your fingers and put them in your pocket or throw them into the closet. Pick up old newspapers, magazines, books, and catalogs and throw them into the closet. Collect socks, underwear, shirts, and pants from floor, chair, doorknobs, etc., and throw them into the closet. Make bed. Whine about your back, have a beer, and, whatever you do, don't open the closet.

3. Tidy up kitchen. Wash enormous pile of dirty dishes and leave them on the dish drain. (Let the air dry them; it doesn't have

anything else to do.) Clean countertops. Fill colorful bowls with Doritos, Tostitos, and all other -itos.

Clutch your heart, close your eyes, and say, "Please, God, not the bathroom."

4.   Tidy up bathroom. Scrub down sink and any easily visible part of toilet. Put out clean towels. Cry. Duct tape shower curtain so no one can open it, ever again, for a million years.

Checklist: Fifth Date

Fluff pillows. Draw drapes. Tell yourself that the thick layer of dust on the lamp shades is "kind of romantic." Close the bedroom door. Wash only the part of the enormous pile of dishes that is higher than the sink. Flush the toilet a few times.

Checklist: Twelfth Date

Fluff pillows. Lie on couch. Stay there until the doorbell rings.

YOU: Oh, I'm sorry. I must have fallen asleep. Darn! I was hoping to clean up a little.

DATE: Oh, that's OK. Don't worry about it. Everything looks … fine.

YOU: Can I get you anything?

DATE: I don't know. Whatever. Do you have any Doritos, Tostito, or … ?

YOU: (reaching between sofa cushions): Yeah, hold on a second …

The Rug

"What is *that?*"

That is precisely, exactly, word for word, what my friend Donna said last week when she finally stopped by to see my "new" apartment, which I've been living in for six years now.

I have roughly twenty good friends who live in Manhattan, and more than half of them have never made the ten-mile trip to visit me in New Jersey because "It's so far, and I don't have a car, and it's so complicated to get there."

So, anyway, Donna finally bought a car, and I finally convinced her to stop by, and I figured we'd go out to dinner somewhere and then maybe come back and watch a movie or something.

But then she finally gets here, and I open the door, and I say "Hi!" and she screams "What is *that?*" and I just about jump out of my skin.

"What is *what?*" I ask. And she points down to my rug and she says, *"That!"* And I say, "It's a rug." And she says, "You didn't tell me you had a rug."

Of course, I have no idea what she's talking about, but I *do* know how stressful it can be to drive through the Lincoln Tunnel, so I rub her shoulders ever so gently and ask her if she wants a drink or something.

"Bill," she says, with this overwhelming sense of urgency, "you have *rugs.* Rugs are *bad.*"

"They are?"

"Of course they are," she tells me. "What's the matter with you? Do you know the chemicals they use to make rugs? Do you know the toxic substances that accumulate on rugs? Do you know that as many as ten million different organisms live in rugs? Do you have any idea what all of these things do to your body? To your respiratory system? To your brain cells?"

I closed my eyes.

This is your brain. This is your brain on rugs.

OK, so maybe we'll go out for a lobster and then *not* come back for a movie.

Maybe we'll just sit on the stoop.

Next thing I know, Donna starts wincing. "I'm already getting a headache," she says. "The toxins are entering my body."

Through her shoes.

"Hey, wait a minute," I tell her. "I've been to your apartment. You have plenty of rugs."

"I have *throw* rugs," she corrects. "Three of them. And they're cleaned once a week. I took all the carpeting out when I moved in there. I have healthy hardwood floors. If I were you I'd rip this thing out before it kills you."

Headlines start flashing before my eyes.

"RUG FLATLY DENIES BEING HOME AT TIME OF MURDER."

"CONSUMED FROM HEAD TO TOE BY WALL-TO-WALL."

"RUG VICTIM'S GAL PAL: I WARNED HIM!"

So, anyway, we go out to dinner, and she talks about rugs for two hours, and pretty soon we both have a headache.

The end?

No.

The following morning the doorbell rings and its the FedEx guy with a package from Donna. So I open it up and there's this paperback book, *Living Healthy in a Toxic World* (Perigee Books, $12) by David Steinman and R. Michael Wisner, with a foreword by Kirstie Alley, the former *Cheers* star and renowned carpeting expert.

On the back are quotes—the kind urging you to read the book— by those other famed toxicologists John Travolta, Tom Cruise, and Nicole Kidman.

Now I may not know a whole lot of stuff about a whole lot of stuff, but I do know that Alley, Travolta, Cruise, and Kidman all belong to the Church of Scientology, which believes that the meek shall inherit the earth and the wicked will spend eternity sorting through remnants and Orientals.

Anyway, there's a bookmark on a page headlined "A Story That Will Floor You." It was about a New England family who became inexplicably ill after purchasing a new carpet. The mother eventually brought samples of the rug to a laboratory "that does tests in which mice are exposed to carpet samples and observed for health effects. When they were exposed to her samples, the mice died."

Hey, fine with me. I *hate* mice.

The authors conclude: "After the family lost their home, fought lawsuits, testified before Congress, and underwent a successful detoxification program, their lives were saved, but they'll never be the same."

In the same chapter I read that I should get rid of the "synthetic" linoleum in my kitchen and replace it with linoleum made from all natural materials.

Which is what?

Do they make cotton linoleum?

So, anyway, I finished my stupid book, and I nosed around my stupid rug, and I took a good look at my stupid self in my stupid bathroom mirror, and I have to tell you, I looked pretty damned good, all things considered: healthy, fit, eyes clear, teeth white, nice rosy glow ...

So?

Obviously, any carpeting that doesn't kill you, just makes you stronger.

That Time of the Month

I'm not crazy about cleaning the bathroom, but I do it, and the job is hardly ever as bad as I think it's going to be.

I'm not crazy about washing curtains, either—because you have to eventually hang them back up—but I do that, too, and it rarely takes as long as I think it will.

So, you wanna know what I *really* hate?

Really, really, really …?

Paying bills.

Dread it. Despise it. Hate it.

First of the month? Hate it.

Writing out checks? Hate it.

Licking envelopes?

I hate it, my tongue hates it, the envelopes hate it.

In fact, there's so much hate swirling around my apartment on the first of the month, I'm surprised the pictures don't fall off the walls.

The problem?

I don't know. On some level, paperwork has always been a problem for me. I'd almost call it a phobia. I see all those envelopes with all those bills in them, and I know I'm in for an absolutely unbearable twenty minutes of ripping things open, licking things closed, adding, subtracting, and check writing.

I don't like writing checks. For one thing, it screws up my bank balance. I write a check to the electric company, the electric company cashes it, and the next thing you know I'm out $38.

I hate that.

The other thing I can't stand about checks is that you have to do all that scribbling. You have to scribble something up there, and something else over there, and something else underneath it, and the whole experience is annoying.

My favorite part of the check is writing my signature, because, oh, I don't know, it's just fun.

My least favorite part is filling out the line where you have to write the amount in words. *One thousand five hundred and twenty-two, 97/100.*

I hate that part. I always have to take a deep breath first. It's like writing a novel.

The part I'm most likely to make a mistake on is the date. I do that all the time. I transpose the month and the day or I screw up the year. Last month, I dated a check 4-1-85, then looked at it, and had to think what year it was. Then I had to write a 97 over the 85. And then I had to initial the change. And then I had to ...

Oh, who has the patience for all this?

After many years of writing out my checks in a thoroughly maddening, disorganized fashion, I eventually came up with a system that I use to this day: I put the bills on one side of the table, and the checkbook on the other. Then I open the bills, throw all the inserts into a pile, and stack the bills neatly. Then one by one, I write out the checks and put them—with the bills—into their respective envelopes and seal them.

Organized, right?

Then—this is my favorite part—remembering that I didn't write anything in my check register, I rip the envelopes back open and start all over again.

Tell me: Do those aliens with the big heads ... the ones who are always flying over Wyoming and crashing somewhere in New Mexico ... do they have to bother with stuff like this? I don't think so. These are civilized people. I can't believe they go running all over the Milky Way on the first of the month looking for a mailbox so they can cover their electric bills and make their flying saucer payments.

So why do I have to do it?

I'm civilized. I have a big head. I'm just living on the wrong planet.

Which reminds me: I used to write my return address on all of those envelopes, but that used to give me writer's cramp, so I bought some of those return address stickers, but I got sick of licking them, so then I got some of those adhesive return address stickers, but I kept forgetting where I put them.

So now I don't put *any* return addresses on the envelopes and, frankly, I don't give a damn.

And I'm willing to bet that my creditors don't care either. Why would they?

They just want my money. They don't care if I live in a houseboat, a possum hole, or a brown paper bag.

Next subject: envelopes.

Envelopes I *love:* the ones that say "No Postage Necessary if Mailed Within the United States."

Love them.

Hate all the others.

I especially hate those envelopes that have ads attached to the back—the ones that you have to rip off in order to put anything inside. On more than a few occasions, I've ripped the ad off, folded it up, and put in into the envelope.

Ha-ha-ha.

It gives me something to do.

I also have an intense dislike for window envelopes. I'm sure everybody was happy, thrilled, and moved to tears, back in 19-whatever it was, when Wilbur and Orville Window invented their wonderful, handy window envelope.

Well, I have news for you: I don't think window envelopes are wonderful or handy. I think they're dumb, because I have to line everything up and shake everything around, and they make me feel manipulated, stupid, and testy.

I also can't believe that it's cheaper to make window envelopes than it is to make envelopes with an address printed on them. I mean, what do the printed ones cost, five cents for two thousand of them?

While I'm venting, I also don't like envelopes that ask you questions.

Did you enclose your check? Did you write your account number? Did you call your mother? Did you put a stamp on the front? Do you think I'm an attractive envelope? Will you miss me when you drop me in the mailbox?

Oh, shut up.

The best part about paying my bills is that I can sometimes put it off for hours, even days. I make phone calls. I find other things to do. In fact, that's when I clean my bathroom and wash my curtains: when I'm *not* sitting in the dining room, paying my bills.

There is a satisfying balance to my life.

My checkbook's another story.

A Tale of Two TVs

Five years ago I bought a big, bad, cable-ready lemon in the television department of a major department store—$525. I can't tell you the brand name. Let's just call it a Ralph Waldo.

Two days after the warranty expired, the entire top third of the screen was filled with lines. I called a repairman. He laughed.

"What's the make?" he asked.

"It's a Ralph Waldo," I told him.

Additional laughter.

I asked if he could come over and take a look at it.

More additional laughter. And a no. He told me to bring it in.

"It's a big TV," I told him. "I drive a sports car. No trunk. No backseat. No can do."

No problem, he told me. Naturally, though, there was a catch: "$40 to pick it up, $40 to bring it back, and $40 to look at it."

If you don't have a calculator handy, that's $120. For what? So he can tell me it needs $400 worth of work? I asked if he could at least give me an idea of what was wrong with it based on my description of the problem.

"Absolutely not," he said. He had to see it in person.

"I'll give you $60 to look at it here," I offered.

"No."

"Seventy-five dollars," I said. "And that's my last—"

"No."

"I'll have it on when you get here. All you have to do is run in, look at it, and run back out again."

"No."

"I'll hold it up in front of the window. Open the drapes. You won't even have to get out of your truck."

"No."

I called another repairman. Same runaround. Same fees. And no, he couldn't tell me what was wrong with it over the phone.

I hung up, walked into the living room, and sneered in Ralph Waldo's direction.

"I spent $525 on you! I have dusted you, polished you, showed you off to my friends, never left you on for extended periods of time … and this is the thanks I get?"

Silence.

"There is no way I am going to spend $120 just to find out what's wrong with you! Do you understand me? I am going to save up for a new TV, and then I am going to throw you into the garbage where you belong. Is that clear?"

More silence.

Not to mention lines.

Fast forward to April 1994: On a bright Saturday morning, I go to a store and buy myself a new television set. Gorgeous. I can't say the brand name. Let's just call it Rhymes with Bony.

I install my Rhymes with Bony where my Ralph Waldo used to be and move my Ralph Waldo over by the coffee table. I then call a neighbor to ask him to help me take Ralph Waldo out to the Dumpster.

No can do, says my neighbor. Ralph Waldo can't go out until Heavy Ugly Trash Day, two weeks from now. Local ordinance or something.

I can't believe it. "Two weeks? But I've got all this company coming over. I can't have this thing in the middle of my living room for two weeks."

"I don't know what to tell you," my neighbor says. "But if you put out any heavy ugly trash today you'll get a summons."

I hang up and call my brother on Long Island. He has a friend with a junkyard. And a truck.

"You think Jimmy could pick up my old TV?" I ask.

"I guess so," my brother says. "But you're in Jersey. You'd probably have to give him $50 or $60."

"Let me get back to you," I say, grinding my teeth.

I hang up the phone, call back the TV repairman, and ask if he wants to buy my Ralph Waldo from me. I'll even give it to him, I say. Just come and get it. He could fix it and sell it. Give it to his mother. Use it for parts.

He asks what's wrong with it. I tell him there are lines on the upper third of the screen—the same thing that was wrong with it three years ago. He then tells me exactly what's wrong with the set, what it would cost to fix, and why it isn't worth it.

All of a sudden he's the Psychic Friends Network.

"If you ever need service on your new set," he adds, "don't hesitate to call."

Thanks.

Small Talk

My brother's Mercedes yells at you. Walk up to the car and she screams, "You are standing too close to the vehicle." Drive around with one of the doors open and she screeches, "Door ajar!" Forget to buckle your seat belt and … I don't know … I think she punches you in the nose.

As my brother was showing all of this to me last weekend, I couldn't help but laugh to myself.

How stupid.

How frivolous.

I want one.

He told me the whole system costs a few hundred dollars—which is a few hundred more than I feel like spending right now. But I wasn't going to let that stop me.

As I drove home, I nonchalantly recited the alphabet just loud enough so my car could hear it.

"A, B, C, D, E, F, G …"

The drive took an hour and a half. I must have recited those same twenty-six letters five trillion times. I talked them, I sang them, I even wrote them in the dust on the dashboard. You'd think that in all that time he would have at least learned a few letters. A vowel. Something.

Well, forget about it.

I went into my apartment, walked into the kitchen, and I guess it was obvious I was depressed. My refrigerator asked what was wrong.

"It's my brother's car," I said. "She's talking now."

The refrigerator smiled. "And she said something that hurt your feelings?"

"No, no. Nothing like that. She just says things like 'Door ajar' and 'You're standing too close to the vehicle!'"

"She sounds charming. You should bring her around here sometime. I could use someone to talk to."

I slumped into a chair. "Please don't start whining again. I put the microwave right next to you. Talk to her."

"Oh please," the refrigerator said. "Not with her attitude."

"It's not attitude," I said, pouring myself a glass of water. "She's just being polite. She's Japanese. It's a cultural thing."

"I guess so," the refrigerator said. "She jabbers away with that VCR a mile a minute. You should only know what goes on here while you're at work."

"Well maybe if you made an attempt ..." I took a few deep breaths, then turned to the microwave and said, "How are you today?"

She lit up. "Very well, Billy-san. And you?"

"Fine, fine. Talk to you later."

The refrigerator was unimpressed. "You call that conversation? I've had more meaningful exchanges with the smoke alarm."

"I didn't know you spoke to the smoke alarm."

"I was just being sarcastic," the refrigerator said. "She shrieks like a banshee."

"Well then ... I don't know. Talk to the juicer."

"He spits. I said hello to him on Friday and got a wad of carrot pulp on my door."

"The vacuum cleaner?"

"Dirty mouth."

I found myself getting edgy. "Then talk to me, dammit! I'm here! I talk! What's on your mind?"

"Well, now that you mention it, I don't suppose the word 'defrost' means anything to you?"

"Oh. Sorry. I've been meaning to get to that."

"And that miserable bag of Tater Tots. What are you saving them for?"

I started rubbing my head. "They're still all right. I need them in case of company."

"Oh, yeah. *Thanks for coming. Have some taters!*"

"And what's with that purple velour cucumber in the vegetable bin? If I've said it once, I've said it a thousand times ..."

"You say *everything* a thousand times!"

"Oh, really? Well, you don't have to worry, mister, because I'm not saying another word to you. Ever!"

"But ..."

"Ever!"

I need to get out more.

The Sneeze

It started with a sneeze. Not even a big sneeze. Just one of those low-to-medium ones.

I was in my living room, sitting on my green-and-white sofa, drinking a cup of coffee, black, one sugar. I had just finished eating dinner. Everything was fine. Not a care in the world.

And then I sneezed.

I held the cup away from me, but it didn't make any difference. I sneezed, my hand jerked, and I spilled some of my coffee on the sofa cushion. It left a small, watery stain about the size of a quarter. And life as I had once known it suddenly came to an end.

As you may know, there are all sorts of people running around who know everything there is to know about stain removal. Chocolate on a shirt, blood on a tie, lemon meringue on lime chiffon—you stain it and they'll unstain it in three or four minutes using milk, ice cubes, hairspray, seltzer, wax paper, peanut butter ... whatever.

I'm not one of those people.

I am fast, though. I ran into the kitchen, put a little Ivory Liquid on a small pink sponge, ran a little water on it, and dashed back into the living room. And in no time at all, my quarter-size stain looked like a map of Argentina. I assured myself, however, that when the water dried, everything would be fine. That night, I turned out the light, went to bed, and forgot about it.

The next morning I woke up, stumbled into the living room, and saw that I now had a dry map of Argentina, and its perimeter was darker than the rest of the cushion cover. Convinced that this was because I had not wet the entire cushion, I went back into the kitchen, got my sponge, filled a bowl with warm water, and sponged down the whole thing. Then I got dressed, went to work, and forgot about it.

When I returned that evening, the cushion cover had dried into a hideous, streaked mess. It was Thursday night; my parents were coming to visit on Sunday. In fact, three days earlier, during the phone call confirming this visit, my mother had said, "I still haven't seen your new couch." (Whenever old Italian women say things like this, you have to immediately spit on the ground, throw salt over your shoulder, make the sign of the cross, and punch a dwarf during a full moon. Otherwise, you're doomed.)

A friend called and I told him of my dilemma. He suggested unzipping the cushion cover and washing it by hand in the sink. "Actually," he said, "maybe you should wash both cushion covers so they don't wind up looking different from each other."

Good idea, right?

I unzipped the covers, filled the sink with Woolite and cold water, immersed the covers, washed them, and rinsed. I noticed that the water in the sink was blue, but Woolite is blue, so I didn't give it a second thought. I just wrung the covers out and hung them up on my shower rod to dry.

About an hour later, when I went in to check on them, I saw these huge cobalt blue stains all over the edge of my bathtub and across my white tile floor. A bunch of thick green threads on the inside of the covers was bleeding bright blue dye all over the place.

What is happening?

I tried wiping up the stains and then draped an old towel along the edge of the tub to catch any more dye that might drip down. I assured myself that all of this would work itself out eventually. There was no way a sneeze and a drop of coffee could destroy my entire house.

On Friday morning, the cushion covers still hadn't dried. A female co-worker told me I was in over my head. "Take them to a dry cleaner," she advised.

"How can I take them to a dry cleaner?" I asked. "They're soaking wet."

"OK," she told me, "then put them in a dryer on the fluff cycle until they're dry."

I went home and followed her advice. When my cushion covers emerged from the dryer, they were fluffy, dry, and blue. Blue like my kitchen sink, blue like my bathtub, blue like my bathroom tiles, blue like my mood.

But maybe not *that* blue. Maybe if I put them back on the cushions, I thought, they won't look so bad. So I put them back on the cushions and—yucch—they looked terrible. Now what? My parents were coming in two days.

I stared at the cushions on Friday night, trying to work up a strategy. Maybe if I left the blinds down in the living room, no one would notice. Or maybe I could replace the white bulb in the lamp with a yellow one. Or ...

Forget about it.

On Saturday night, I had a sudden inspiration. I got some baby powder from the bathroom and started chucking it all over the cushions. I let it sit for a while and then wiped it off gently. I could see an improvement almost immediately: The powder had significantly lightened the blue. Hmm ...

I tossed more powder on the cushions. Then a little more. Then a little more, until the entire container was empty. When I was done, I realized the cushions didn't match the rest of the couch exactly, but they were close enough. All I had to do was keep the drapes drawn, throw some pillows around, and no one would notice.

Am I a genius or what?

Feeling celebratory, I poured myself a glass of Chianti and plopped myself down on the sofa, causing a white mushroom cloud to billow out from under me.

Then I sneezed.

The Postmodern Host

In her 1922 best-seller *Etiquette,* Emily Post warned that throwing dinner parties is "not for the novice." Had she left it at that, we'd probably be a lot better off today. But no, she went on and on, intriguing us with all this fancy talk about proper invitations and tasteful introductions, what fork goes where, which glass goes with what beverage, and where the servants are supposed to stand once the soup's been dished out.

Post died sometime thereafter—long before it became fashionable to tell your guests they had to chip in for the pizzas, get their shoes off the coffee table, and pipe down so you could hear the bones cracking on *Cops.*

I suppose it's safe to say that dear, departed Emily's been spinning like a propeller ever since.

Personal experience has taught me that the worst thing about inviting people for dinner is that they usually take you up on the deal. Beyond that, the joys of being a host are a mixed bag. For confirmed novices, a crash course follows:

Q: How far ahead is it proper to invite guests for dinner?
A: There is no precise answer to this question, and it doesn't matter anyway. If you can get them on the phone before they've actually made their dinner, they'll probably have their fat butts on your stoop within ten minutes.

Q: Is it a good idea to ask my guests what they'd like to eat?
A: It's nice—but rarely advisable. If you don't ask, they'll probably eat whatever you throw in front of them. Ask and you're likely to find out that Bob's a vegetarian, Chuck's macrobiotic, Lulu's allergic to milk products, and Troy hates shrimp, beef, pork, lamb, garlic, onions, and mushrooms. (Trust me on this one: People named Vinny, Joey, and Tony eat whatever you put in front of them. People named Troy are nothing but trouble.)

Q: Many of my friends have young children. Is it wrong to invite the adults, but not the little ones?

A: Dinner is not a meal for children. Chances are that by 8 P.M. they've already had breakfast, lunch, and enough Twinkies, Yodels, and Ding-Dongs to put the average adult on life support. More food will only make them puffy and surly and give them nasty nightmares.

   Of course, if you make your intentions clear, and your guests bring their children anyway, by all means greet them graciously at the door. Just make sure that you close the door before any of the children manage to slip in. While you're at it, secure any other entrances you may have, latch the windows, and release the Dobermans. Should you feel bad about this, remember that locking children outdoors teaches them valuable foraging skills and stimulates their tender young imaginations.

Q: Is it impolite to ask guests to help out in the kitchen?

A: Generally speaking, guests enter the kitchen only when everything is going smoothly. They stand in your way, cause you to walk into cabinet doors, ask you extremely idiotic questions, and make all sorts of distracting small talk. ("Oh, you put vinegar on your salad? What a clever idea.")

   On the other hand, if everyone's in the living room chatting and you call out for assistance because you need something from the refrigerator, the pots are boiling over, smoke's pouring out of the oven, and your pants are on fire—trust me, no one will pay attention until you run past them with a wet towel over your head, screaming like Robert Wagner in *The Towering Inferno*.

Q: I don't have a dishwasher. Is it acceptable to give my guests plastic cups?

A: Plastic cups are functional, and many are now quite attractive. I try to give the guests their own plastic cups shortly after they arrive and tell them to hold on to them all night or I'll bust their kneecaps. You can even serve hot beverages in plastic cups providing you instruct your guests to gulp them down quickly before any messy meltage occurs.

Q: Is there a nice way to tell guests you prefer to clean up by yourself?

A: On television, people are always inviting other people to dinner and making these delightful five-course meals in bright, happy kitchens the size of the men's department at Bloomingdale's. The guests help chop the celery, set the table, and clear the dishes; there's plenty of counter space; nobody ever bumps into anyone; and the whole place is spotless five minutes after the meal is done.

In real life, few of us have kitchens large enough to accommodate every well-meaning, freeloading slob who feels like wandering through. Unfamiliar with your way of doing things, guests will often pile plates onto one another—making it necessary for you to wash both sides of the plates, instead of the one side you were counting on. They will also put items in the refrigerator precisely where you don't want those items to be—it may be months before you ever see that ketchup again—and furtively toss silverware into the bubbly waters of your sink, causing you to lacerate your hands in several places.

"Madge, where's that carving knife?"

"You're soaking in it."

If a guest insists—as some do—that she has to clean something "or I'll just feel terrible," hand her some Ajax and point her toward the bathtub.

Should the guest decline that offer—as some do— politely tell her to get her fat butt in the living room with everybody else and shut up till the coffee's ready.

The Long, Thin Table

A couple of weeks ago my friend Donna invited me to her place for dinner and I noticed something new in her living room: a long, thin table covered with framed photographs of friends and relatives.

This is a popular thing all of a sudden: My friend Jane has one. My friend Rich has one. My cousin Louise has one.

Apparently, all you have to do is buy a long, thin table, pick up a bunch of frames, stuff the frames with photos, arrange them at artsy angles, and the next thing you know, you have a whatever-you-call-it.

Of course, the minute you do this, folks will start coming to your house, looking at the pictures, asking "Who's this?" and "Where was this taken?" and wondering why you don't have a picture of *them* sitting there.

People can be so selfish and childish and stupid.

My brother and his wife Joyce keep one of these tables in their TV room. It's long and thin and covered with pictures of *her* family and pictures of *my* family, but mostly pictures of *her* family.

This is explainable, in part because there are only six people in my family—three of whom are Joyce, my brother, and their daughter—whereas Joyce has a mother, a father, a stepfather, three brothers, two sisters, and twenty-one nieces and nephews.

I'm not the jealous type, but I guess it bothers me that she has all these pictures of *them* on her picture table and only one picture of me.

When I was over there on Memorial Day weekend, I kinda, sorta moseyed into the TV room and kinda, sorta stood by the long, thin table, and—even though I'm not the jealous type—I kinda, sorta took a head count.

There were three photos of her mother, which I think is a little excessive, including one in a silver, heart-shaped frame. But there were also three photos of her brother Chris, two of her brother Al, two of her brother Anthony, and one picture with all three of them in it, right up front, in an expensive gold filigree frame.

How nice for them.

Now I'm not the jealous type or anything, but I was a little put off by the fact that their group photo was right up front in an expensive gold filigree frame and mine was in a cheap, plain, black frame off to the side, lying face up, with a glass of iced tea on it.

See? This is one of the chances you take when you visit someone who has a long, thin table of pictures in their house.

Joyce's brothers are right up front in a $75 frame and I'm a coaster.

Or, rather, I'm a coaster *when I'm visiting.* When I'm not visiting, they probably keep me on the kitchen counter so they can lay hot lasagne pans on my face.

"Joyce? Where do you want me to put this lasagne to cool?
"Oh, just lay it on that picture of your brother."

Later that night back at my parents' house, I did another head count, even though my mother doesn't have a long, thin table of photos. Not yet, anyway.

She hangs her pictures on a wall in her den.

So there I went, and there they were, directly over the television set: a big photo of my niece Talia, flanked by two double frames. In the double frame to the right were two pictures of my brother as a child. In one he's wearing a straw hat. In the other he's playing a guitar.

In the double frame to the left were two pictures of me as a child. In one I'm smiling directly into the camera. In the other I'm sitting next to ... my brother.

I didn't have a guitar. Although I asked for one on several occasions.

Now I'm not the jealous type or anything, but I couldn't help but notice that I was in two pictures and my brother was in three pictures.

I suppose it would have been selfish, childish, and stupid of me to bring this to anyone's attention, so I didn't. I just kept my mouth shut, took my brother's double frame down, and hid it behind the television.

Before I left, I was tempted to mention how I felt about all of this.

Back at my apartment all of my photos of all of my friends and relatives are in a big plastic bag in a drawer in my desk.

I don't have them in gold filigree frames.

I don't have them hanging on a wall.

I don't have them artfully arranged on a long, thin table.

And that, after all, is how things work in this country, isn't it? Sure it is: I scratch your back; you scratch mine.

Joyce probably goes to her brothers' houses, sees pictures of herself all over the place, and then goes home and puts out more pictures of them.

How two-faced, hypocritical, and desperate for attention can you get?

The next day, I ran over to my neighbor Rich's apartment to take another look at his long, thin table and to ask him where I could buy one.

I've never been two-faced or hypocritical, but I can't remember a time in my life when I wasn't desperate for attention.

As soon as I walked into his living room, though, I noticed that all the photographs were gone. The long, thin table was covered with cards.

"Is it your birthday?" I asked.

"Tomorrow," he told me.

"Oh, I'm sorry," I said, shaking his hand. "I forgot. Happy birthday!"

I then walked over to the long, thin table, and I have to tell you, there must have been fifty birthday cards there. I couldn't believe it.

"There are only about forty of them," Rich said, "but the mail didn't come yet today."

I'm not the jealous type or anything, but I've never gotten that many birthday cards in my life. In fact, the only person who actually *mails* me a birthday card is my dentist. Everyone else just hands me one when they see me.

Rich found this odd. "You mail cards to them, and they don't mail cards to you? That's so rude!"

I shook my head. "No, I never send out cards. I'm not too good with stuff like that."

"Well, then, what do you expect?" he asked. "If they don't get cards from you, why should you get cards from them?"

Do you see what I mean? This has nothing to do with love, caring, or sentiment. It's all about politics, collusion, and what's-in-it-for-me.

Whatever you do, don't tell my dentist.

Modern Living

Accountant at the Wedding

My best friend's niece (and godchild) is getting married on August 28 on Staten Island, with a reception to follow in Brooklyn. I happened to mention this to my neighbor Richie, who comes from a big family and goes to more weddings than anyone I've ever known. I haven't been to a wedding in six years. He's been to five this year alone.

"Including my cousin's," he told me. "June twenty-sixth. It was his second marriage in three years. The first one lasted one year and three months. This one lasted six days. They came back from Aruba two days early. She didn't want to be married anymore. I told them I wanted my check back."

I thought he was kidding me.

"I'm *not* kidding," he told me. "Three hundred dollars for six days? No way. And a second marriage? Forget about it."

"Why did you give so much?" I asked. "Three hundred dollars is a lot. I thought it was $75 a person."

"Where have *you* been?" he asked. "In '76 it was $50 a person. When I got married in '82, it was $75. One of my friends gave me $25. I couldn't believe it. I'm still shaking the envelope. From '86 to '90 it was $100, now it's $150."

"Really?"

"Of course. A good hall charges $125 a person. And you want to give them more than that, don't you?"

"I guess. But $300 sounds like a lot of money."

"Well then you use the formula," he said. "Not every wedding is $125. Some are more. Some are less. You see when you get there. Don't write out the check till you're going to give it to them. Then when people start going up to give them the presents, you go in the toilet and write it out. Bring a pen. If you forget, just knock on the next stall and ask one of the uncles for one."

"But how do I know how much?"

"Well, she's not a relative, and you're not married, so right there, it's $150 for you and $50 for your date. That's $200, if everything's good. Are you following me?"

"Yeah."

"OK. You walk into the reception, you check the place out. Plastic flowers and fountains, you deduct. Plastic flowers and fountains, you know you're in trouble."

"Really? I didn't know that."

"Of course. Then you go to cocktail hour. Knishes, hot dogs, frozen stuff—you deduct. If it's not an open bar, you deduct. Last year I was at one at the Holiday Inn on Route 46 … knishes, no mixed drinks. Forget about it. I thought I was at a ball game. Frozen stuff and no open bar, take out $15. But if you see a macaroni table, a seafood table … all those things, you add $25."

"Yeah, but doesn't that take away from the idea of a gift? I mean …"

"Gift shmifft. This is a formula. It was set up by your ancestors. Don't screw it up. It works. Now after the cocktail hour, you go inside and see where you're sitting and who you're sitting with. Maybe you should write all this down …"

I got some paper.

"OK," he said. "Sitting too close to the band, you deduct $15. Sitting by the kitchen, deduct $25. Then count the number of tables you are from the first table and deduct $10 for every table in between.

"OK, next is the food. Prime rib, add $35 a person. Choice of three, add $50. Chicken, you deduct. Broiled chicken, boiled potato and mixed vegetable, you just give them $10 and go home. Don't even make an excuse."

"But I like chicken," I told him.

"Doesn't make any difference," he said. "This is a wedding. Just shut up and keep writing. Rolling bar, add $15, but only if there are enough of them. Figure one rolling bar for every 50 people. Otherwise, you deduct.

"Plus, look at the centerpiece. Is it worth taking home? All the aunts fight over it 'cause they want to take it to the cemetery the next day. Just ask your date if she likes the flowers, and then figure it that way. Carnations—nothing. Those big red ugly things that look like they're from another planet, you add. Although, personally, I hate them.

"Next is dessert, and listen carefully here. Venetian Table, take out $30. Venetian Hour, with all the liqueurs and the pastries, and the sparklers on top, add $45. Bad Venetian Hour, add nothing, unless the bride's mother is crying and the father is arguing with the manager in the front office 'cause he spent so much money and everything stinks. That breaks my heart.

"A good band, you add. If you make a request, say you want to hear 'Mala Femina,' and they don't play it, deduct $10. If you ask for 'Mala Femina' and they never heard of it, deduct $45. Is the bride pregnant?"

"I don't think so."

"Well, times are changing. That used to be *disgraziada*. Now it can go either way. But if she's showing and wearing white, deduct. If she's showing but says she isn't pregnant, deduct $50. If you think the baby's gonna be out before the thank-you cards, deduct $20 and save it for the christening."

I was scratching my head. "But ... what if you go and the food's bad, and the bride's pregnant, and you're sitting with people you don't talk to ... and you still have a great time?"

"No buts," he said. "You still go by the rules. You say, 'Would my grandmother pay $200 for broiled chicken and a bowl of boullion?' I don't think so. When did you get this invitation, anyway?"

"Last week."

"Last week?" He started counting. "Hey, you're in luck! That's only five weeks. You don't even have to go. You're on the B-list."

"But they invited me on the phone last year when they got engaged."

"Oh, really? And they're not even related to you? Well, that's great. That's an honor. Add $50, right off the bat."

"I add for that?"

"Oh, yeah. Sure. Definitely. But keep your eyes open."

Gimme a *B*

I'm sitting with a bunch of desperate women who are chain-smoking, cursing, and sloshing down caffeine. Their faces are careworn; their eyes fiery and intense. Addiction has taken its toll on most of them and made it difficult for them to concentrate on anything else. Husbands have fallen by the wayside. Children have learned to make dinner for themselves. As the night wears on, you can see the tension building and the agony that occurs when someone else raises her hand, jumps to her feet, and screams at the top of her lungs ...

"BINGO!"

A man rushes to her side, inspects her card, and yells out to the caller: "Seven! Twenty-three! Fifty-two! Seventy-one!"

The caller looks at his lightboard, nods, and says softly into the microphone, "That's *goooood* BINGO."

Others in the hall clear their cards in disgust, light another cigarette, and mutter a mix of obscenities and idle threats. We're doing lapboards next—those are the thick cardboard grids—and going for the Indian star—an *X* through the card plus all the *N*s. That's a $75 pot, in case you're interested, and a total of $1,000 in prizes over the course of the night, between the lapboards and the specials. (Specials are color-coded sheets of newsprint, six games to a sheet.)

Buy some chances at a dollar a pop and you'll have a shot at the 50–50 drawing. Half the money goes to the winner; the other half goes to the church.

So—you know—God won't mind. After all, this isn't moneylending we're talking about. It's just a pleasant blend of gambling, coveting, false idols, dirty gestures, and good, strong coffee.

I am sitting in the gymnasium of St. John's in Bergenfield, New Jersey. Bring your BINGO chips, your BINGO wand—a magnetic contraption that sucks up chips like a vacuum cleaner—and whatever else you need to pass the time. Arrive early for the best seat, whatever that means. Sit close, far away, toward the stage, or away from it. Sit in the bathroom if it feels lucky. This isn't a hockey game, Myrna. This is BINGO. Everything you do, you do for luck. Wear your lucky sweater, kiss your lucky statue, rub your lucky brooch, and thank your lucky stars that if you don't win on Wednesday, there's always Friday, or Sunday, or—get this—there are even BINGO weekends where you can go on eight-hour binges and play till you explode.

You can bring your husband, your boyfriend, or your son, but warn them that women outnumber the men 50 to 1. Maybe it's just as well. Men aren't tough enough for this sort of thing. BINGO, like childbirth, requires a certain grit that doesn't fall under the jurisdiction of testosterone.

It's my first time—can you tell?—and my friend Rochelle, who has brought me to this den of iniquity, points out all the regulars: the woman with the troll dolls rubberbanded together in naughty positions, the other one who sits right under the lightboard so she can give the finger to the caller, the man who rings a cowbell every time the number 69 comes up.

The coffee urn is through those doors in that smoky little alcove under the crucifix. The bathrooms are just past the alcove. The non-smoking section is, literally, in the next room, but it's filled with smoke anyway. Smoking, from what I've been able to gather, is part of the pathology, along with all the lucky charms and the bumper crop of bumper stickers flowering in the parking lot: "I brake for BINGO!" "Grandma's on her way to BINGO!" "Point me to the nearest BINGO!"

As we assemble our boards, Rochelle tells me I'm going to win. "It's your first time," she says. "First-timers always win." And, secretly, I think she's right. I won my first time at Aqueduct, OTB, and Atlantic City, and even picked up $48 the first time I played the lottery. Still, I assure her that winning isn't important. I just want to have a good time. And when the woman two tables down wins $60 for getting the plus sign—that's all the Ns plus the middle horizontal row—I cheer her on.

Three games later I still haven't won anything. I haven't even come close, but maybe that's understandable. I'm only playing three cards at a time. Some of these women use thirty cards at once, and they attend to them with the precision of air traffic controllers.

It's time to make an X on our boards—and waddya know? The same woman who won the plus sign gets the letter X and another $60. I cheer her on one more time, though less enthusiastically.

Two more games go by and I'm purchasing additional boards just for the hell of it. I'm also crossing my fingers, reciting impromptu prayers. I even ask the woman with the troll dolls to let me rub their little Day-Glo heads.

Game 16 is the "Coverall" and the first person to fill an entire board wins $200. Deep down I know I'm going to win this one. All my boards are cooking. I feel good. I only need two more numbers to win and I know it's going to happen.

But—damn you, BINGO man!—it doesn't.

Excuse me, I'm getting a little emotional.

The same woman who won the plus and the X also wins the Coverall. I smile politely but I have begun to hate her.

When it's time for the 50–50 drawing the man with the drum chooses me—the only virgin on the island—to pick the winner. "It's your first time," he says. "Make someone very happy." And I do as I'm told.

God's work, I think they call it.

A woman at the next table claims the prize—$316 in cold hard cash, including $5 of mine—and jumps up and down. I hate her, too.

The game breaks up around 10 P.M., two hours after it started. Boards are collected, chips are dumped methodically into bags and cake tins, and women who have refused to get up at any point during the evening rush to the bathrooms.

In the crisp night air of the parking lot, some pleasantries are exchanged, and people who were sneering at each other earlier in the evening do some last-minute bonding.

The total damage on my end was just under $10, along with the painful realization that my first-time lucky streak has finally been thwarted. Would I do it again? Oh, I don't know. Doubtful. Probably not. Are you kidding? Nah.

Why? What's the point?

Oh, OK. See you Wednesday.

Fast Food

I'm gonna try to make this fast.

On Saturday, I was running all over creation, and I was supposed to meet some friends in Manhattan at 6 o'clock. But by 4, I still hadn't eaten, and I was really running late, so I drove over to Roy Rogers and …

Wait. Before I tell you that, let me tell you this: There was a time—way back when—when fast food was *fast*. And by fast I don't mean: Coming right up, or any minute now, or just a second, I'll be right back. I mean: *fast*. I mean: You told them what you wanted, and they gave it to you. I mean: You gave them the money, and they stuck the hamburger in your mouth. I mean: *fast*.

That's why they called it *fast* food. Because it wasn't slow. It was *fast*.

It was also cheap, but that's another story.

So, anyway, I went into Roy Rogers and …

Wait. Before I tell you that, let me tell you this: I know fast food was fast because, believe it or not, I used to work in one of these places. (I can't tell you the name for legal reasons, but it began with an *M,* and it ended with a *cDonald's.*) It was 1972, and I was what used to be known as a bunman. Bill the Bunman.

My job—if you want to call it that—was to stand in front of a toaster all day, sliding sesame seed buns into the toaster and then sliding them out again. Then I'd slide more in, and I'd slide more out, and I'd slide more in, and I'd slide more out, and I did this for eight hours straight, five days a week, for six consecutive months, until it finally occurred to me that if I didn't leave I was going to wind up in an insane asylum, hooked up to an MRI machine.

You know how an MRI machine works, don't you? They slide you in, and they slide you out, and they keep staring at pictures of your brain until they find something unusual.

"Bill, we've found a shadow in your lower cortex. We can't be sure, but it looks like … a hamburger bun."

I mention all of this because I don't want any unhappy mothers calling in and telling me how their poor little Steven—or their poor little Jennifer—spends untold hours toiling over a bun toaster, or a burger grill, or fillet o'fish-o-matic, sweating, tripping on grease puddles, and making absolutely nothing.

Because I've toiled and I've tripped and I've been there.

I know.

So, anyway, I go into Roy Rogers, and I order these two dinky roast beef sandwiches with the small soft drink, and I pay this poor little Steven the $7.77 and *I'm in a hurry.*

So poor little Steven asks me if I want some Happy Meal or whatever they call it, and I say no.

So he asks me if I want some fries with my order. And I say *no.*

So he asks me, "How are things in Glocca Morra?" and I say *no.*

No.

No.

Two roast beefs, and one small drink, and *that's it.*

Let's *go!*

Well, it turns out there's only one roast beef in the roast beef bin, so Steven orders another one. *And I wait.* And it doesn't come up, so he orders it again. *And I wait.* So now there are people on either side of me getting their chicken sandwiches and their mashed potatoes, and *I'm waiting,* and they eat and they leave, *and I'm waiting,* and people who weren't even *born* when I got there come in and buy their McRoy Burgers and their Trigger McNuggets, *and I'm waiting.* And finally poor little Steven shouts, "I'm still waiting for that roast beef," and poor little Steven's fat little boss says, "OK. Cool it."

Did you get that? Did you hear it? Do you want to write it down?

"OK. Cool it."

Ugh.

So another eternity goes by, and some other man walks in and orders a roast beef sandwich, and some other poor little Steven walks over and takes *my* roast beef sandwich out of the bin while *my* poor little Steven stands there, dumbfounded, and I'm telling you, if I had a shotgun, I would have pulled it out and killed every last one of them.

So I ask *my* little Steven for *my* money back, just as *my* second roast beef slides down the chute. So he calls *his* manager, and she calls *her* boss, and I yell at *her,* and I yell at *him,* and as far as I'm concerned they can bring out Roy, Dale, Tonto, Zorro, the mayor of Muffinland, and anyone else they've got back there *because I want my bleeping money back!*

So, *finally,* I get my bleeping money back, and I get in my bleeping truck, and I drive next door to bleeping Burger King, and I go up to this poor little Steven, and I ask for a Whopper and a small soft drink. And he asks if I want a meal—and I don't—and he asks if I want some fries—and I don't—and asks if I want cheese and I say no. *I just want a plain bleeping Whopper.*

So I pay poor little Steven $3.65 and I then proceed down the counter to poor little Jennifer, who gives me my sandwich, and then I sit down, and I open it up, and it's this piece of meat with no lettuce, no tomato, no mayonnaise, no nothing.

So I go back to poor little Jennifer and I open the bun and I say there's nothing in here, and she says "You ordered a plain one." And I say, "He asked if I wanted cheese and I said no; I wanted it plain." She then rolls her eyes and says "Oh, God! That's not plain! That's regular!" and proceeds to give me all this bleeping *attitude,* like I really want to have another argument over another six cents worth of chopped meat.

Sensing that I am a difficult customer, she tosses the plain thing in the trash and gives me a new one, and I finally sit down, and I finally eat, and I finally get back in my truck and ... that's the whole story.

Fast, wasn't it?

Check It Out

It's 7:30, I've been working all day, and I just filled a shopping cart with $110 worth of groceries in just under fifteen minutes. I'm good. I'm fast. I'm organized.

And now I must be punished.

Mind you, I'm smarter than the rest of these grocery suckers. I don't just go on any old line. I know which clerks are slow and which ones aren't. I can tell which customers will bag their own and which ones won't. I can peruse the cart of the people ahead of me and automatically compute the ratio of canned vegetables (which can be scanned) to fresh (which require the clerk to look up coded numbers in a book hanging from the register, enter the code onto his keyboard, and then weigh them, like I have all night).

Within seconds I choose the line that will have me out of the store in the least amount of time, using a foolproof mathematical formula of my own design.

"I'm closed," a listless clerk tells me.

"Oh, I'm sorry," I say, throwing a can of olive oil at his head. I now have $99 worth of groceries, but who needs all that fat?

I continue The Search, finally settling on counter 5. There are only seventy-seven shopping carts in front of me but I feel good about this. I assure myself I'll be out of here in no time.

The people on my line are all reading about Elizabeth Taylor's amazing liposuction and Lisa Marie's incredible ordeal with Michael. They're not paying attention to what's going on around them. They're soft.

But I'm no fool. There are four unmanned counters and someone just paged Kevin.

I don't know who Kevin is, and I don't know where Kevin is. But in my heart of hearts, I know Kevin is going to open. I can feel it in my bones. And I'm going to be there *first*.

Slowly, inexorably, I back up my cart. Not a lot, just enough so that when Kevin plops his drawer into the register, I can *bolt*.

Three counters down, I see a woman who has even more in her cart than I do, and she's backing it up in the exact same way. But I throw two rib steaks at her head and she falls to the floor. What an arm! I now have $92 worth of groceries.

I know there's no way in hell that Kevin's going to say, "Can I have the *next* customer, please?" Nobody does that anymore. Kevin's just going to plop in that drawer, turn on that little overhead light, and say, "Open."

And I'm gonna be there. Yeah. And there won't be anyone ahead of me to screw things up with a charge card, or a big bag of coffee that needs to be ground, or some weird brown gourd that isn't in Kevin's little vegetable book.

"Could someone get me a price on this?"

No sirree. Kevin's just gonna plop in that drawer and I'm gonna be there, tossing all my junk on that hot little conveyor belt. He's gonna scan it and I'm gonna bag it, and then I'm outta here—1–2–3.

Precious minutes pass. Finally I see a young man in a white shirt walking toward the courtesy desk, and I *know* it's Kevin. He talks to the girl with the blond hair and then walks away, without a drawer. As he passes, I ask if he's Kevin.

"No," he says. "I'm Steve."

"Oh, I'm sorry," I say, throwing a carton of Tropicana and four LaYogurts at his head. I now have $86 worth of groceries.

Another young man walks by. "Are you Kevin?" I ask. "No, I'm Bernie," he tells me in a hail of Ronzoni.

"Are you Kevin?" "No, I'm Mark."

Garbanzo beans everywhere.

It's 10:30, there are only thirty-five carts in front of me, and all the men in the store are unconscious, including Kevin, whom I hit with a jug of Clorox by mistake.

But I'm optimistic. Someone just paged Laurie. And after years and years of grocery shopping, I really feel I have this all down to a science.

Men's Fashion: A Primer

It's that time again. Should I or shouldn't I?

Men know what I'm talking about. We all know when we're over-due for some new clothes; we just don't want to have to go out and get them.

Oh, there are exceptions, of course. If you gave my father a mil-lion dollars and said, "Take this to the mall and spend it all on shoes," he'd say, "No problem," and be back in an hour and a half with a mil-lion dollars' worth of shoes, slacks, tie clips … whatever you told him to get.

My father *loves* shopping, trying things on, mixing and matching.

I *hate* shopping, trying things on, mixing and matching. (Although I generally mix pretty well, I don't match with any noticeable suc-cess.)

But I'm thinking about getting some new clothes, which is at least a step in the right direction, isn't it? A couple of shirts. A couple of ties. New pants. Jacket. The end.

So I pick up this men's fashion magazine—always a mistake—and I notice the actor Kenneth Branagh on the cover, and right away I start panicking. Kenneth is wearing a navy-blue pin-striped suit with wide lapels, a blue-striped shirt with a white collar, and a gold tie. He is unshaven, his hair is frosted, and except for his rather distinctive sculpted nose, there is nothing in this picture of him that I want to own.

So then I flick through the magazine and soon realize a couple of things. First, muscular bodies are in, but so are emaciated bodies. All of the models look as if they either work out eight hours a day or have expensive heroin habits.

Like most American men, I'm somewhere in between: My arms, chest, and legs look as if they have an expensive heroin habit and my stomach looks like a Budweiser commercial.

But enough of this. I'm not going to fall into *that* trap. I'm not going to stand in front of a mirror and hate myself because I'm not muscular or emaciated, or because I don't have a Roman nose and a cool haircut, or because I don't have shoulders like a linebacker, or a gymnast, or, well, *any* shoulders.

This is all a plot, you know. Fifteen years ago they did this big study and determined that women *hated* their bodies and men *loved* theirs, and sociologists went on and on about how horrible this was and how we have to do something about it. Well, apparently we have. Now everybody hates their bodies, no matter who they are or what they look like.

Anyway, I continue flicking through the pages, and the next thing you know, I'm seeing a lot of uniforms: army looks, navy looks, drabs, khakis, boots, buttons…. Uniforms are in, too. Hmm …

I sort of like this. I think. And then I browse a little more and see this story about uniforms in which the author explains, "Uniforms are an easy look for men to understand. They just have to know what to do with them."

Well, OK, so what *do* you do with them? I mean, outside of putting them on, taking them off, and sending them to the cleaners once in a while?

Turns out that uniforms require "a sure sense of style; an understanding of construction and silhouette; a flair for accessorization; a compelling philosophy."

See? This is my problem. I get up in the morning and I don't have a compelling philosophy, at least until my third or fourth cup of coffee, and by that point I just want to get the hell out of the house.

I do see some truth in this, though. I mean, have you ever noticed any time you see a bunch of cops standing around that some of them look really good in their uniforms and some of them don't?

I'm sure they know this themselves. I'm sure when they're in their locker rooms, holstering up, they talk about stuff like this, man to man.

"Hey, Mike, I don't get it. Your uniform always looks so good on you. And mine … I don't know … it just *hangs.*"

"I'm not sure what to tell you, Bruno. Maybe blue isn't your color."

"It's not just that. I'm beginning to think the whole silhouette is wrong for me. It's just not flattering."

"Bruno, you're making too much of this. I think you look very smart. Although ... if I could make a suggestion or two ..."

"Please!"

"Well, you might want to try wearing your gun a little more to the left."

"Oh, really? You mean ... like this?"

"Exactly. And move your billy club more to the center. Let it follow the line of your trousers."

"Hmm ... interesting. How's that?"

"Fabulous! Makes all the difference! You look just like Richard Gere in *An Officer and a Gentleman.*"

"Oh, stop!"

"No, really. Now, tilt your hat forward a little ... little more ... little more. That's it! Perfect! Really accentuates your eyes! Yes! You look stunning!"

"Thanks, Mike. It means a lot to me."

"Bruno, I'm telling you, accessorization is everything. Accessorization, a sure sense of style, and a compelling philosophy. Incidentally, you look *really* good in hats. Have you ever thought about becoming a fireman?"

"Once or twice. Why?"

"Well, I could really see you in those wide brims. And the silhouette on those coats is, let's face facts, a knockout. Plus, the suspenders would accentuate your upper torso ... give you a great V shape. And they come in red!"

"That's true. And I really do look good with a little splash of color. It lights up my whole face."

"I'm sure it does. Of course, so does fire."

"Hey, six of one, half a dozen of the other."

"Too true, Bruno. Too true."

The Get Well Card

A co-worker drove up to Vermont with her husband last weekend for four romantic days at some rustic bed-and-breakfast. She was sitting on the bed—and had yet to have breakfast—when she blacked out.

She spent the next seven days in some rustic Vermont hospital bed—no breakfast here, either; she had a perforated ulcer—and I was naturally concerned, shocked, saddened, so on, so forth, etc.

I was just about to send her one of those perky pick-me-up bouquets when yet another co-worker approached me and said, "We should collect some money for Nan."

Notice the wording, here: "We" should.

I grimaced, and said, "Yeah ... well ... OK. Let's do it."

A message was quickly posted in the newsroom. It said, in effect, that Nan had suffered a perforated ulcer while on vacation in Vermont. A collection was being made to send her flowers. Please give money to Bill or Ginny. Period.

This sort of thing is done all the time when someone has a baby, or someone dies, or someone gets engaged, or someone sneezes, or someone does whatever else they have to do to deserve a happy, peppy, floral pick-me-up, and one of those big FROM ALL OF US cards with all those goofy animals on it.

"Heard you're sick! Get well quick!"

I've been through this half a million times already, but it never gets any easier. Being the money collector doesn't mean that people run over to your desk, throw down some cash, and then run in the other direction. Being the money collector means you actually have to *talk* to all of these people. Even if you don't want to. Even if you're two hours late with your column. Even if your editor is yelling at you to stop talking and start typing.

"God! I just saw the message! What happened to Nan?"

"She's ill. In some hospital in Vermont. Perforated ulcer. Desperately needs flowers. Wanna give some money?" *Type, type, type.*

"You're kidding! What happened?"

No sooner do I finish the whole bed-and-breakfast, sitting on the bed, blacked-out story than someone else comes rushing over.

"What happened to Nan?"

"Ill. Vermont. Perforated ulcer. Flowers. Money." *Type, type, type.*

"You're kidding! What happened?"

Bed-and-breakfast. Sitting on the bed. Blacked out. *Type, type, type.*

"You're kidding! That happened to my aunt once! She had gone to New Hampshire and blah-blah-blah, blah-blah-blah, blah-blah-blah."

Kathy enters, stage right. "What happened to Nan?"

"Ill. Vermont. Perforated ulcer."

"Oh, that's terrible! Is she OK? What was she doing in Vermont? Was she on vacation? Does she have a history of ulcers?"

"How much are you contributing?"

"Three dollars."

"Sorry. That's all you get for $3."

An exasperated Mary Lou rushes over, near tears. "I can't believe it," she wails. "I was just talking to her on Friday!"

"That's probably what did it. Where's your cash?"

Teresa, shell-shocked, can't believe it, either. She begins to recount all the sad things that have happened to Nan during the last fifteen years.

Tom comes over and explains, for twenty minutes, that ulcers are caused by a virus.

Ed has ulcers, but they aren't perforated.

Bob had a perforated ulcer, but he's never been to Vermont.

Jill's going to Vermont and would like to stay at a bed-and-breakfast.

For the next hour there are thirty people huddled around my desk talking about ulcers, flowers, bed-and-breakfasts, whether or not the Devils will leave New Jersey, pottery, politics, continuing education, who did what for July Fourth, where they're spending Labor Day, and what brand of aspirin they use.

My editor rushes over frantically to ask how I'm doing.

"Almost done," I tell him.

"What are you writing about?" he asks.

"Ill. Vermont. Perforated ulcer …"

Poetry in Motion

When their Teflon expires, women don't yell or panic or do crazy things. They just go out and buy new frying pans. Men in the same situation act a little like lab rats on experimental drugs. We become frustrated, disoriented, restless; we hang our heads, walk into walls, eat imaginary cheese, and so on and so forth.

My last nonstick frying pan, which no longer has its nonstick surface, came with a "lifetime guarantee." I bought it only seven years ago, but I guess that's seventy in frying pan years. According to tradition, this pan should have moved to Miami in 1988. It should be sitting out by the pool right now with all the other elderly kitchen utensils … taking it easy … going to pot parties … stuff like that.

Sure I'm sad. The breakup was difficult. One day my food was gliding across the pan like poetry in motion. ("Is that Dorothy Hamill," my guests would inquire, "or a potato pancake?") The next day it was like I didn't exist. The pan had no respect for me whatsoever. Eggs were sticking, onions were sticking … things that had never stuck to anything else were sticking to the bottom of my pan.

And it wasn't just that my eggs were sticking. It was *how* they were sticking—like these two big, yellow eyes staring up at me.

Defiantly.

I was heartsick, flabbergasted, and more than a little ticked off. I still have shirts from college, socks from high school, and my first pillow. The first pillow from my first bed. So this business of going out every seven years and buying a new frying pan doesn't exactly sit well with me.

Besides, the rest of the pan is fine. The bottom still looks good. The handle's still firmly attached. The cooking surface still has that healthy, lifeless gray color.

But the damned thing doesn't work.

As Emily Dickinson observed when she went through a similar ordeal:

"Ah, gentle frying pan, warmed by fuel!

"Thy bottom noble, thy surface cruel!"

After accepting the fact that I could not live with a nonstick pan that sticks, I decided to go to the store to buy a new one. While I was there, I figured I might as well pick up a new fan for my living room. This is another tale of woe, but what am I supposed to do? I can't lie and tell you what a happy person I am when my household appliances are tearing me up inside.

Every year I buy a new fan, and every year it breaks, and every year I go to the store to buy another one, and so on into infinity.

When my last fan started making these rude sputtering sounds a couple of weeks ago—days before my frying pan turned on me—I felt that same twinge of betrayal Al Pacino felt in *The Godfather, Part II* when he realized John Cazale was the traitor in his family.

"You broke my heart, Fredo," Pacino said, kissing Cazale's cheek.

It was very moving. Unlike my fan blades.

Eventually, my old fan wound up in the Dumpster. So did my old frying pan.

Same day. Same Dumpster. Sad? Sort of. When I walked into my apartment with my new fan and frying pan I looked over my shoulder and saw the old ones gaping at me.

I felt bad for them, but what could I do?

My new fan cost $29.99. Interestingly, my new frying pan cost $29.99, too. I'm sure this is just some bizarre coincidence. But maybe it isn't. Maybe it means something. Maybe it's a sign, an omen, or something weird like that.

As Emily Dickinson once observed:

"Ah, gentle fan: sleek and slinky!

"Same price as pan! Co-inky-dinky?"

Knot Amused

What tie-wearing man hasn't ventured into a store on his way home from work and heard those annoying, four little words?

"Don't you work here?"

It happened just yesterday. I had gone to the A&P and was waddling up aisle 7 with my four jugs of Deer Park water, when this woman walked up to me with one of those in-house advertising fliers in her hand.

"I'm looking for these paper towels," she said, "but they're not where the other paper towels are."

"I'm very sorry to hear that," I told her as I waddled toward the cash register.

"Well, where are they?" she demanded, slapping the flier against her cart.

"How the hell should I know?" I asked.

"Well, don't you work here?"

"No!"

"Oh. I'm sorry. You look like you work here."

"Well, I don't."

I'm not generally so huffy when someone makes a mistake about something. But I've been dealing with this particular mistake since I was eighteen years old.

It's happened in hardware stores:

BIG GREASY MAN:	Do you know where the glue guns are?
ME:	I think they're over there somewhere.
BIG GREASY MAN:	Well ... don't you work here?
ME:	No.
BIG GREASY MAN:	Oh. I'm sorry, guy. You look like you work here.

It's happened in clothing stores:

SMALL PUSHY WOMAN:	I have to return these pants and there's no one in that department.

ME:	Really? I hate when that happens.
SMALL PUSHY WOMAN:	What are you—a comedian? I hate this crummy store!
ME:	Excuse me?
SMALL PUSHY WOMAN:	Don't you work here?
ME:	No!
SMALL PUSHY WOMAN:	Oh. I'm sorry. I hate this crummy store so much. You look like you work here.
ME:	Thanks. So do you.

The reason for all of this insanity, of course, is my necktie—a thin shard of fabric that goes around my neck and hangs down in front of my chest. (And what a clever idea that was. I'd give anything to have seen the look on people's faces when the guy who invented ties tried explaining to people *why* they should wear one.)

My friends tell me they have the same problem.

One said he always tries to remove his tie before entering a store, because it's such a—you'll pardon the expression—pain in the neck. ("People see a tie," he said, "and then come flying at you like homing pigeons.")

Another told me he was approached in a fast food restaurant one day by an angry woman who thought he was the manager. When he said he wasn't, she said, "Well, what are you wearing a tie for?"

A third, my friend Steve, said he was once in a large department store and was approached by a very dapper gray-haired man who was apparently the store manager. There were other customers standing around in need of assistance, and the manager scolded him for not going over to help them.

"You're kidding me!" I said. "What did he say when you told him you didn't work there?"

"I didn't tell him," Steve explained. "I took off my tie, said, 'I quit!' and walked out the door."

If they gave awards for this sort of thing, Steve would have definitely won.

Or at least tied.

Is It or Isn't It?

The nicest thing I can say about turkey bacon—aside from those favorable fat and cholesterol percentages—is that it *smells* like real bacon.

In fact, it smells a whole lot like real bacon.

In fact, while you're eating it (as I am doing as I write this—Butterball Thin & Crispy to be exact), you may even find yourself thinking that someone nearby—a friend, a relative, a next-door neighbor, perhaps—is sitting down to a hot steaming plate of *real* bacon while you are sitting down to a hot steaming plate of ... whatever this is.

Come to think of it, what *is* this, anyway ...?

Hmm ...

"Ingredients: turkey, bacon flavor (rendered bacon fat, smoke flavor, cooked bacon), water, salt, sugar, sodium phosphate, sodium erythorbate, autolyzed yeast, sodium nitrite."

To tell the truth, I've never heard of a third of those things, and I can't even find "autolyze" in the dictionary.

Is "autolyze" a new word or some little joke over at Butterball?

BEN BUTTERBALL:	We can't tell them what kind of yeast we're *really* using, so maybe we oughta lie about it. Hey ... oughta lie ... autolyze. That's it!
BEN BUTTERBALL, JR:	But, Pop, what if someone looks up "autolyze" in the dictionary?
BEN BUTTERBALL:	Who'd do a thing like that?
BEN BUTTERBALL, JR:	Gee, Pop, I don't know. Maybe some reporter somewhere. What would I tell him?
BEN BUTTERBALL:	Benny, if you want to run this company someday you'd better stop talking like an idiot and start talking like a Butterball.

I had no such problems last year when I was strolling through a health food store and picked up—are you sitting down?—Nature's Sausage.

Ah yes, Nature's Sausage.

Isn't that an evocative name? Perfect for a *National Geographic* special.

Join our team of bold explorers as they comb the world for ... Nature's Sausage. Tonight at 8 on TBS.

Produced by a company called Fantastic Foods, Nature's Sausage is some sad, gray, powdery stuff that you mix with water. You then let it sit for an hour or so, form it into a "sausage-like patty," and cook it.

Doesn't that sound delicious?

Actually, I tried making these things a couple of times—in an effort to cut down on my pork, fat, and cholesterol intake—but the stuff, tasty as it might have been, was so damned gloppy that my patties fell apart. Someone later suggested I add flour and eggs to the mixture, which worked just fine. The only problem was that by the time I was done, my Natural Sausage patties had more cholesterol than real ones do.

Oh, that Mother Nature. Such a kidder.

Should you care, the ingredients for Fantastic Foods' Nature's Sausage are: "brown rice, textured vegetable protein (soy flour), dehydrated vegetables (yellow peas, green peas, potatoes, garlic, onions), gluten flour, sesame seeds, barley, bulgur wheat, yeast extract, dried yeast, spices, sea salt, brown rice syrup powder, soybean oil, and paprika."

No autolyzed yeast, as you might have noticed, but maybe that's the problem.

Maybe autolyzed yeast is some top secret culinary stealth missile that holds all this goo together.

> FRED FANTASTIC, JR.:   Dad, I really feel you're being short-sighted here. As I think these reports prove, without a shadow of a doubt, autolyzed yeast is the future.

FRED FANTASTIC, SR.: I don't like the sound of it.

FRED FANTASTIC, JR.: But, Dad, all our market research indicates that...

FRED FANTASTIC, SR.: Freddy, if you want to run this company someday, you'd better start talking like a Fantastic and stop talking like a Butterball!

Well, as it turns out, autolyzed yeast—according to my source at the U.S. Department of Agriculture (USDA)—is really just "a flavoring agent for a number of meat and food products. It is rich in vitamin B and has a strong savory flavor."

That didn't sound so bad. I then asked her what "autolyzed" meant.

"I honestly don't know," she told me. "But autolyzed yeast has been recognized by the Food and Drug Administration as a GRAS substance."

GRAS?

What does GRAS mean?

"Generally recognized as safe."

Oh.

Beulah, peel me a pork chop.

The Wristwatch

Seven years ago I bought a wristwatch with a narrow, rectangular face and a handsome brown leather strap. I brought it home and used the flat, little knob on the side to set it. I then wore it two or three times before placing it in my sock drawer, where it remains to this day along with five or six handkerchiefs, a pair of black shoelaces, a couple of stray buttons, and a yarmulke.

At least my socks know what time it is.

Watches don't do much for me. (Ditto for rings, bracelets, and gold chains.)

So, naturally, friends think I'm a little crazy: "Where's your watch?" "How come you don't have a watch?" "I could never get through the day without my watch. How on earth do you manage?"

How on earth do I manage ... *what?* Telling time? What kind of question is that?

Did Julius Caesar wear a wristwatch? (No.)

Did George Washington? (No.)

And I know for a fact that the Hunchback of Notre Dame didn't wear one either, but he always managed to ring that bell on time. At least I think he did. Not that it would have mattered much. I mean, if he was three minutes late, would anyone have known the difference?

Life was so uncomplicated in those days. People got up at dawn, went to bed at dusk, and ate when they were hungry. No one rushed home on Tuesday to catch *Frasier.* And if you were three days late for a job interview, nobody batted an eyelash. (On the other hand, if you happened to casually mention to someone that it was 3:17, you would have been excommunicated, tried for witchcraft, and burned at the stake.)

Who cares what time it is? Watches make me nervous.

Anyway, seven days ago, I received a gift. A wristwatch. Digital. With a round face and a black rubber strap. I accepted it begrudgingly, but tried to appear as enthusiastic as possible: "What a nice watch! Look at that! Just what I needed! Thank you, thank you, thank you!"

That night, after slipping under the covers, I took my new watch out of its box and gave it the once-over. According to my new watch, it was 11:13.

According to my old VCR, it was 12:05. Hmm ...

I got out of bed and walked into the kitchen, where it was 12:10 on the wall clock and 12:07 on the microwave. Then I walked into the living room where it was 12:03. Then I walked into my office where it was 8:30.

I stumbled back to my bedroom, tripped over something (the international dateline?), and turned on the weather channel.

It was 12:13:52 A.M.

So I picked up my watch and reached for the flat knob on its side so I could set it. But there was no flat knob. Just four buttons. So I reached into the box and pulled out the "Easy Directions"—seven pages long—which included a diagram of the watch face that identified the buttons as A, B, C, and D. Like I really needed this at 12:13:52 A.M.

Well, OK, let's see: You have to hit D to go from twenty-four-hour alarm mode to dual alarm mode to chronograph mode to ninety-nine-minute timer to dual time mode and then, finally, to normal time mode.

Once you're in normal time mode, you hit A to make the seconds flash, and then you hit B to advance the seconds.

Then you hit A to make the minutes flash, and you hit B to advance the minutes.

Then ... well, you get the picture.

Of course, by the time you're done with this, everything *but* the year has changed, and you have this overwhelming desire to hit A with a sledgehammer and B with a monkey wrench.

As I later found out, my new watch has an hourly chime and a watch face that glows in the dark. It also has a stop watch—in case I ever have to judge a marathon—a wakeup alarm, thirteen computer chips, four-wheel drive, whistles, rockets, a tomato slicer, and, according to the box, "a sleek, sophisticated look that goes everywhere!"

Hmm ...

Sock drawer.

On the Road

Directions

Last weekend, I missed a co-worker's wedding in the Bronx because I made a wrong turn off the Major Deegan Expressway and wound up in Canada somewhere.

Stopping at gas stations used to get me out of messes like this. But nowadays there are only two English-speaking gas station attendants in the entire country, and they both work at a Getty Quik Mart in Idaho.

Today when you're lost, you have to depend on the kindness of strangers—the majority of whom completely ignore you, either because they think you're going to rob and kill them or because they want to rob and kill you, but there are too many other people around.

Truth be told, I come from a long, unbroken line of short Italian men who get lost pulling out of their driveways … and I'm not quite sure why. Is difficulty with directions a genetic thing? Or learned behavior? Or both?

Certainly, much of my rudderless childhood was spent in the backseat of a wayward Dodge Dart yelling "Are we *there* yet?" while my father drove around in circles, tapping anxiously on the dashboard, and saying things like "I think that sign looks familiar."

Dad, it *should* look familiar. We've passed it seventeen times already.

On the day of my first holy communion, we actually had to stop for hamburgers *on the way* to the restaurant where we were supposed to have lunch, because "Wrong Way" Emilio couldn't find the restaurant where we were supposed to have lunch. After an hour and a half of wrong turns, I was so hungry I began chewing on the upholstery like a starving dachshund.

Twenty years later, while visiting a friend in Virginia, I took a little drive to Washington, D.C., with detailed directions on how to get there. On the return trip—"Just follow the directions backward!"— it suddenly occurred to me that I was lost, because the roads didn't look familiar, and the stores didn't look familiar, and because the last sign I'd read said WELCOME TO BALTIMORE—YOU STUPID IDIOT MORON.

Two years ago, at the conclusion of my second trip to D.C., I spent well over an hour trying to find my way out of the city. I finally pulled into a gas station, where I hooked up with a carload of New Yorkers, also lost. An attendant gave me and the other driver very careful directions in ... I don't know what it was—Portuguese?— and fifteen minutes later we all wound up back at the same gas station.

"Now what?" the other driver asked me.

"I don't know," I told him, completely exhausted. "Maybe we should just send for our things and move here."

I did make it to the wedding *reception* last weekend, but missing the actual wedding made me realize it was time to seriously think about this problem, and confront it honestly. After considerable thought I came to the following conclusions about myself:

1. Has no sense of direction. (Does know up from down, but that's about the extent of it.)
2. Doesn't listen. (Feigns attentiveness, nods frequently, but has no idea what you're talking about. Is sure he can get by with a few key words such as "turn," "keep going," and "look for the pizzeria.")
3. Has tendency to confuse left with right. (Prefers person in passenger seat to fully extend arm in one direction or the other, and say, "Go *that* way.")

4. Is bad with maps. (What's the point of looking for where you're going when you can't find where you already are?)
5. Would rather stay home and sleep than go just about anywhere, do just about anything, see just about anyone.

A few years ago, convinced that my father was never going to change, my mother assumed the role of direction taker. And a couple of days before they visited me for the first time in New Jersey, she insisted I give the directions to *her.* When I asked why, she said, "Because I am your father's eyes." I told her that was very nice, although I generally prefer the person with the eyes to be the same person who does the driving.

In her new role as Vice President in Charge of Going Places, my mother was a taskmaster. "I want *exact* directions to there from Long Island," she barked. "I don't want *any* problems."

When I told her the name of an exit, she demanded to know the number. When I told her to drive a few miles, she demanded to know the exact distance. When I told her "three or four lights" she demanded to know if it was three *or* four.

And when I told her to drive across the George Washington Bridge, she demanded to know which direction they were supposed to head in: "Are we taking it north, south, east, or west?"

"Ma, it's a *bridge.* You take it to the side you aren't on."

On the way to my house, when they passed a sign for my town that was before the turn I had told them to make, my mother told my father to turn. And, of course, they got lost. Later, when I asked why she did that, she said she'd just assumed that I had made a mistake.

"How could I make a mistake giving directions to my *own* house?" I asked.

"Are you kidding? Your father does it all the time."

I'm doomed.

Wild Things

There is no question that as a teenager, I went out of my way to turn both my parents into nervous wrecks: staying out all night, growing my hair down to my shoulders, playing Beatles records (backward) at all hours.

Now—God love 'em—they're returning the favor.

True to form, my mother called my office last week and told me she and my father were taking a little trip. "We're going down to Florida," she said.

"Oh, that's nice," I said nonchalantly. "Do you need a lift to the airport?"

"We're not taking a plane," she informed me.

"Dock?"

"We're not taking a cruise," she replied.

"You're not taking a pack mule down there, are you?"

"We're driving," she said—almost haughtily, now that I think about it. Naturally, I hit the ceiling. "Driving? What do you mean 'driving'? When? How?"

"We are old enough to drive," she reminded me.

I told them they were crazy. "Why can't you fly?"

"We don't want to fly," she insisted. "We want to drive. We've been cooped up in this house all week. I can't stand it anymore."

I reminded her that she was preparing to be cooped up for three or four days in a car. With my father. "And you don't even like him."

"Look," she said, "we want to take a trip, and we've never been to Florida. So we're going."

"You've never been to Paramus, either," I told her. "You don't come visit me in Jersey 'cause it's too far. Now you're going to Florida. For what? There's nothing to do down there."

Then it hit me: It was spring break. My two spindly, wrinkled, ricket-ridden old parents were going to Florida the same week as spring break. I closed my eyes, saw them dancing in wet T-shirts on MTV, and a shiver ran down my spine.

"It's a mob scene down there," I told them. "Are you crazy?"

She told me they weren't going all the way south—just as far as Orlando. "We're going to Disneyland and EFCOT," she said.

"It's Disney World and *EPCOT*. You don't even know where you're going. EFCOT? Why are you doing this to me? You know Dad's terrible with directions. And you're both blind as bats. This is crazy. I won't let you go."

Everyone I know—friends, co-workers, you name it—told me I was being overprotective. "Plenty of senior citizens take trips like that," one friend informed me. "Leave them alone. Let them have fun."

Oy.

The fun couple left the next morning, promising to call my brother or me at some point, "while we're on the road." Doesn't that sound cute? On the road.

I'd like you to meet my parents, Hope and Crosby Ervolino.

Two days later, my brother called to tell me that my parents were in Georgia, were doing fine, and would call me the next night to check in.

That night I arrived home at 7, sat by the phone, and waited for the call. And waited. And waited.

At 10 P.M., I called my brother. "They didn't call me," I said. "Did they call you?"

"No, I haven't heard from them," he said. "They probably spent all day at Disney World. I'm sure they'll call later."

By 1 A.M., they still hadn't called. I was pacing around the house like a lunatic. Where the hell are they? They always call when they say they're going to call. They know I'm worried. They know I have no idea where they are. Even if they were too busy to call, they could have at least … I don't know … called and told me.

The next morning, I wanted to call the police.

"What police?" my brother asked. "We don't even know where they are."

"Any police! I don't know. Georgia? Florida? Maybe their car broke down. What if they got a flat? What if they joined a religious cult? What if they spent the night stuck on Space Mountain, going around and around, screaming for help, but no one heard them because their voices are so tiny and old?"

I put on CNN just in case. I switched to MTV, but there was no sign of them. I called the travel channel and asked if there really was an EFCOT somewhere.

That night, they finally phoned and said they were tan and fine and having a grand old time.

"Why didn't you call me last night?" I demanded.

"Oh, I'm sorry," my mother chirped. "We forgot."

Forgot?

Forgot?

Go have parents.

New Jersey Drive

My friend Chuck called last week. "I was just wondering: If I took the bus out to Jersey on Saturday, could you drive me over to Home Depot? I need to pick up this special paint they have."

No problem, I told him. "There's one in Paramus. I went there a few months ago."

Not necessary, he said. "There's another one right near you in Secaucus. I can see it from the bus."

I didn't know that. "Well, OK. Try to come around noon. I'll run you over there and then I can drive you back to the city. Shouldn't take long. We can have lunch downtown."

"Great."

No, not great. One thing I forgot about New Jersey: Just because you can *see* something, doesn't mean you can *get* to it.

On Route 3 he tells me, "Get over to the right. I think it's coming up."

I get over to the right and drive onto the off-ramp.

"Yeah, there it is," he says. "Over there on the left."

I saw it!

At the end of the ramp are two signs, SECAUCUS on the right, NJ TURNPIKE on the left. I'm going 50 miles an hour, heading right.

"*No!*" he screams. "It's on the *left!*"

I screech to the left. I can still see Home Depot. But I won't see it again till the moon comes over the mountain.

Life on the New Jersey Turnpike is smooth and leisurely. You don't have all those distracting exits to worry about. When I finally do see one, I pull off.

At the toll plaza I explain my dilemma to an understanding clerk. "Take the second exit," he tells me, "and get back on the turnpike."

I take the second exit and get back on the turnpike. Heading south. "I think we're going the wrong way again," I say to Chuck.

"Well, then get off," he says.

We get off. We get on. We go here. We go there.

An announcer explains: *These are the voyages of the* Starship Enterprise. *Their seven-year mission is to buy paint in Secaucus.*

We're now in someplace called Jersey City. There are signs for north, south, east, and west. Chuck wants to know what direction we have to go in. I tell him, "I don't even know where we *are.*"

We follow the traffic for more than twenty minutes, past burned-out buildings, salvage yards, bodies lying in the street. There are no signs anywhere, but I'm pretty sure we're someplace in Chicago.

The next thing I know it's 1:30. We've been driving for an hour and a half. You'd think that in all this time we'd at least pass *another* Home Depot.

Eventually, we see a sign for the Lincoln Tunnel. Close enough. We head toward it and get onto a ramp that curves into infinity, like some gigantic DNA molecule. There's swamp on either side of us. I want to get out and have a good cry but Chuck says, "I think I just saw a crocodile."

On Route 3 we head east to the tunnel and then get off at one of forty-seven exits that says Kennedy Boulevard. We drive past a Toys R Us, and make a left, so we can turn around. But there's an accident on the other end of the street, and the traffic is being diverted. *To where?*

We drive another three or four blocks. A cop moving the traffic asks where we're going. I burst into tears.

Twenty minutes later we're back on Route 3 heading toward Secaucus. Chuck sees the Home Depot again, looming like the Lincoln Memorial. "Do you really have to go inside it?" I ask. "Can't you just tell your friends back home that you *saw* it?"

The next thing I know, it's right in front of us.

"We're here!" Chuck screams.

"Don't get cocky," I tell him. "We're not in the parking lot yet. Anything can happen."

But through some divine intervention, Our Lady of the Lost Jersey Motorists guides us into the lot.

"Thank you, most generous lady," I say as she floats back into the clouds.

Half an hour later, we're on our way out, heading for Route 3. We can *see* it.

Three or four wrong turns later and we're heading back to Jersey City.

Chuck is screaming. "Who *built* this place?"

Forget it, Jake. It's Chinatown.

Partly Sunny, Chance of Reindeer

It was too cold in New Jersey last week, so I took off for Florida, where everything is air-conditioned: houses, cars, stores ... no matter where you go in the Sunshine State there's always an arctic gust waiting to blow down your back or up your sweatpants.

At my friend Scott's house in Fort Lauderdale every room, except for the screened-in "Florida room," was so chilly I had to bundle up in sweats and flannel.

"Hey, I've got an idea," I said to Scott on Tuesday. "Why don't we open the windows today and let in some fresh air?"

He looked at me like I was crazy.

"Oh, come on," I pleaded. "It's freezing in here."

"No," he insisted. "If we open the windows, the house will become too humid and it'll take hours for the air-conditioning to correct it."

"But ..."

"No."

In the car, it was the same thing. I'd climb in, see the AC ducts pointed at my chest like a firing squad, and freak.

"Scott, it's only eighty degrees outside today," I told him. "Can't we open the ..."

"No," he said. "My hair will frizz."

"Oh."

People with hair are such a pain in the ass.

Once I settled into the swing of things, the highlight of my mornings was waking up, making coffee, and then running outside and sitting on the lawn.

After lunch on Wednesday I returned outside with a large towel and camped out on the grass with some sunblock and a big glass of ice water. I closed my eyes.

I oohed and aahed. After dealing with 30-degree temperatures over the Thanksgiving weekend, it was great to feel the warmth caressing me.

"This is so nice," I told myself. "It's summer again."

I started drifting off, dreamily conjuring up images of candy-striped beach umbrellas, kids splashing in the surf, couples slathering each other with tanning butter, the Beach Boys singing "Help Me, Rhonda …"

Then out of nowhere, I heard Christmas carols.

I looked up and discovered that the people across the street were decorating their house.

The Mr. had this huge cardboard box of plastic sleighs, cherubs, and Santas that he was dragging across the sand like Lawrence of Arabia.

The Mrs. was stringing white lights around the base of a palm tree.

And from the opened garage door I heard Bing Crosby crooning about how he was dreaming of a you-know-what.

Yeah, Bing? Keep dreaming.

From where I'm sitting, you're looking at sunny, mid-to-upper 80s, 20 to 30 percent chance of showers.

But despite the weather, this couple was intent on turning their home into a winter wonderland, even at the risk of sunstroke, hyperventilation, third degree burns, and frizzed hair.

Incredible.

As the holiday tunes kept pouring out of the garage, the house was gradually transformed into a sparkling Christmas card by Currier & Ives, with a postmark from Gilligan's Island.

Dripping with sweat, the Mr. and Mrs. retreated into the garage for iced teas, and Andy Williams started singing "It's Beginning to Look a Lot Like Christmas" as sleigh bells tinkled in the background.

Hey, Andy, does the word "denial" ring a bell?

After another hour or so, the heat index had climbed to 94 and I couldn't take it anymore. I eventually returned indoors, wrapped myself in flannel, and sat shivering on the couch while the couple across the street put the finishing touches on their house and then ran back inside.

At around 3 P.M. a ripe coconut fell on the lawn, missing Santa Claus by inches, and I noticed that Rudolph's back was redder than his nose.

So was mine.

Too hot outside. Too cold inside. But if you ask anyone from the northeast why they moved to Florida they'll tell you the same thing: the weather.

I don't get it.

A Bathroom in Paris

A few days after I arrived in Paris, the international edition of *USA Today*—one of my few links with the Stars and Stripes—ran a story saying that Americans favored exotic travel destinations. There was a catch, though. As one travel agent explained, "When we take U.S. travelers to Europe, I see more people who are low-key, more flexible, more interested in learning what a foreign country is about. But they still want American bathrooms."

Another agent agreed. "Americans love American bathrooms," he said. "Let's face it. Our plumbing is the pinnacle, and we know it."

I thought this was interesting because, let's face it, I never knew our plumbing was the pinnacle of anything. I didn't even have a clue.

When I arrived at my friend Chuck's apartment—a two-room flat which, like almost everything else in Paris, was built before World War II—I had no idea what I was in for. It was a chilly morning, about 40 degrees, and I hadn't slept a wink on the plane. All I wanted was a hot shower and a place to sleep for a couple of hours.

"Where's the bathroom?" I asked.

Chuck escorted me into the bedroom, where I found a plaster rectangle the size of a tool shed. I opened the door and there it was: no window, no rug, no mirror, and a 25-watt yellow light over the sink. Not only was there no heat in there, but the floor was paved with hexagon-shaped bricks. It was freezing.

Lined up side by side, starting from the right, were the toilet, the bidet, the sink, and the ... something.

"What is that?" I asked, pointing to a small white plastic vat.

"That's the bathtub," Chuck told me.

The "bathtub" was about three feet long and a little less than two feet wide—perfect for washing a small child or a bag of dirty socks. It had a seat, no curtain, and a shower hose. Just above it, riveted to the wall, was a hot water tank that looked as though it could crash to the floor at any moment.

"I don't get it," I said.

Chuck then demonstrated proper tub usage for me, although he didn't use any water because there were three of us staying there and only enough hot water for two showers. So we had to conserve.

"First," he told me, "you turn on the hot water and spray the tub, so it isn't so cold. Then you turn off the water. Then you sit in the tub and hose yourself down and turn off the water."

He got into the tub to show me how comfortable it was. His chin was touching his knees.

"Then you soap yourself up, hose yourself down, and turn off the water. Then you're done."

Done?

He said I wouldn't be able to wash my feet because there wasn't enough room to move around. "To clean your feet," he told me, "fill up the bidet about halfway with warm water, stick your feet in one at time to get them wet, then soap them up, and rinse them off. Then you can wash your face in the sink, shave, and you're all finished."

I started crying.

"Oh, come on," he told me. "There's nothing to it. You'll get used to it in no time." He then handed me a towel and left.

Convinced I didn't need a shower all that badly, I brushed my teeth and called it a day. By the next morning, though, everyone in Paris knew it was time for me to take a shower. I didn't have any choice in the matter.

After three cups of coffee and lots of frantic pacing, I finally went into the bathroom, took a few deep breaths, and began.

I filled the sink and the bidet halfway with hot water, took off my clothes, and hosed down the tub. Then I closed my eyes and climbed in.

I sprayed myself down, just as Chuck had told me, and began shivering. I turned on the hot water again, but my hand was wet, and I couldn't turn it off.

I looked up and saw the hot water tank shaking so violently that the rivets were popping.

Try to picture this: You're nude. You're shivering. And right above you, a hundred-pound tank is about to fall into your lap.

I finally shut off the water and grabbed the soap, which slid out of my hand and flew across the room. Cursing, I jumped out of the tub, hopped across the ice-cold bricks, retrieved the soap, and jumped back into the tub.

Afraid to use up any more hot water, I reached over to the sink and used the hot water in there to lather up the soap. I soaped myself from head to ankle—no easy task when you're sitting down; and reaching your feet really is impossible—and then turned the hot water back on. The spray went everywhere: the floor, the walls, under the walls, into the bedroom …

"What are you *doing* in there?" Chuck screamed, when he saw the thin stream of water flowing out from the bathroom.

"Go @#!% yourself!" I screamed back.

I twisted the knob, jumped back out of the tub, threw some of the warm water from the sink onto my face, and grabbed the towel. Then I hopped across the cold bricks to the bidet, where I put my right foot in, took my left out, did the hokey-pokey, and turned myself about.

I shivered, quivered, howled …

"This is *insane*," I said, as I pushed the door open. "I felt like a duck jumping from puddle to puddle! What *is* this? How can you *do* this every day?"

Chuck rolled his eyes and said, "You don't know how lucky you are. I've seen some of the other bathrooms in this neighborhood and mine is better than all of them put together."

Yeah. It's the pinnacle.

Apple Blossom Time

I returned to Amsterdam to find it much the way I'd left it in December, with only a few slight alterations, the most notable—still in progress—at Prinsengracht 263, better known as Anne Frankhuis, the seventeenth-century canal-side house where Anne Frank and her family spent more than two years in a cramped attic, hiding from the Nazis.

The house, one of the city's most popular tourist attractions, was overrun with construction workers the entire time I was in Holland. When I asked my friend Rolf what was going on, he said—are you sitting down?—*they're making it bigger.*

Bigger?

"All right guys, let's get these dormers up ..."

Is this an idea or what?

"To your left is Anne Frank's Jacuzzi, as well as the master bedroom, library, home entertainment center ..."

No, no, no, Rolf insisted. They're not making the *attic* bigger; they're constructing an annex that will eventually be transformed into a war museum.

Just the mention of the word "war" made me cringe.

Europe doesn't need a war museum. Europe *is* a war museum.

As we traveled over the next few days through the south of Holland, Belgium, and Germany, I was keeping track of the activities of the U.S. armed forces in the Persian Gulf. At night on television, I'd see missiles flying everywhere and all of those ominous stealth bombers taking off into the wild blue yonder.

During the day, through the windows of our rented, dented Mazda 626, I'd see incredibly old buildings stranded in the dense shadows of hastily built skyscrapers, some beautiful, some not.

Either way, they serve as constant reminders of what was and wasn't left standing after the war. In Belgium, the quirky juxtaposition of old and new haunts the streets of Antwerp.

Rotterdam wasn't nearly as lucky.

"The Dutch surrendered in five days," Rolf explains. "Rotterdam was completely destroyed. The Nazis were going to bomb the entire country. We had no choice."

Amsterdam was spared the bombs as well as the trauma of modernization. As a result, it remains impossibly—and irrevocably— quaint, a fairy tale maze of ancient row houses that are separated from the canals they overlook by narrow one-lane streets. (It remains one of the world's few major cities in which bicycles outnumber cars.)

On our trip back from Cologne and Belgium, Rolf drove me to Limburg to see the house where he was born and the nearby cemetery where his grandparents are buried. Then as we headed back toward Amsterdam, he popped the question: "Do you want to meet my parents?"

Long pause.

"Oh, I don't know," I shrugged. "Are they anything like my parents?"

After a hasty phone call - "Come for lunch", Mama Eussen urged; Papa was still at work—we headed to a town called Geleen, and the four-story house where Rolf's parents—Mary and Joseph, thank you very much—have lived for the last thirty-three years.

When we got there, Mrs. Eussen was outside in her garden, reading some Dutch tabloid that was littered with stories about Princess Stephanie—whom she likes—and Princess Diana—whom she doesn't.

"Every hour Diana puts on a new dress," Mama exclaimed.

"I know, isn't it awful?" I replied—even though that's one of the reasons I like her.

In June, Rolf had made a splendid impression on my parents. And even though Mrs. Eussen and I spoke different languages, I was determined to do the same.

Maybe too determined. In the first ten minutes I told her that her garden was beautiful, her hair was beautiful, her dining room was beautiful, her hallways, her rugs, the tiles in her kitchen … I couldn't shut up until she said something to Rolf in Dutch, and Rolf turned to me and said, "Shut up."

But lunch was great: homemade chicken broth laced with parsley and scallions, a platter of salmon salad with sliced tomatoes and hard-boiled eggs, followed by salami, cheese, and black bread, followed by tea, followed, an hour or so later, by coffee and plum tortes.

We went out for a walk afterward at a nearby shopping center, where I found an Andrews Sisters CD and bought it for Mrs. Eussen. She was thrilled. "You know the Andrews Sisters?" she asked. I told her I only knew Maxene.

Her eyes lit up. She had meant, "Do you know *of* the Andrews Sisters?" That I had actually met one of them seemed unimaginable to her.

We spent the rest of the afternoon dancing in the living room to "Bei Mir Bist Du Schon" and listening to Mama's stories. During the war, when she was fourteen, Mrs. Eussen was part of a troupe that entertained American soldiers. She sang, danced, and recited poems.

The south of Holland was liberated by the Americans (the north by the Canadians and the English) and tears welled in her eyes when she told me how she felt when they saw the Americans coming into their town: "We knew it was over; we knew we were safe."

She also told me of a cemetery in Margraten, the final resting place for thousands of American soldiers whose families could not afford to have their bodies brought home. She "adopted" one of the graves at the end of the war, and every year since then she has returned on Memorial Day and on the dead G.I.'s birthday to place flowers there. Through the years, she's also corresponded with his family.

Imagine listening to this *and* "Apple Blossom Time" simultaneously.

When she dies, Mrs. Eussen told me, someone from her family will continue to honor the grave.

"They died to free us," she told me. "We will never forget."

Mental Anguish

A Freudian Slip

I *accidentally* shaved my head last weekend, and I still don't know why. Things like this just sort of happen to me. They've happened before. They'll happen again. I have this tendency to … I don't know … get carried away.

My only hope is that years from now, long after I'm gone, someone with a strong psychiatric background will gather all of these columns, read them very carefully, and put together the shattered mosaic of my sad and tortured existence. As a humor writer. (Hmm … compensation anxiety?)

Interestingly enough, this story actually begins with my mustache. I've had it for years. In fact, as soon as I could grow one, I did. But two years ago, on a lark, I decided to shave it off, just to see what I'd look like without it.

Call me impulsive.

I locked myself in the bathroom—odd, when you consider that I live alone—and proceeded to work myself into a lather. A few hasty maneuvers with my razor (whoosh, whoosh, whoosh—displaced aggression?) and I was done. I washed off the foam, looked into the mirror, and almost had a heart attack.

Looking back at me was the face of my father. (Dissociation phenomenon? Multiple personality? The Three Faces of Bill?)

It was all there: the Emilio nose. The Emilio lips. That sharp Emilio cleft between the nose and the lips. During all those years I'd trimmed my mustache, clipped my mustache, combed my mustache, and even waxed my mustache—obvious obsessive-recurrent behaviors—it never occurred to me that my father was lurking underneath it, itching to get out.

And I let him out. I was him. And he was me. I had released my inner parent.

My father, myself.

In a panic, I turned away from the medicine cabinet and ran out of the bathroom. (A typically Freudian response: attempting to conserve equilibrium by abolishing disturbing stimuli.) I knew I had to be imagining things. That mirror was too small. I was focusing too much on that tiny space between my nose and my mouth. It couldn't really be that bad. So I went into my bedroom where I have a full-length mirror, looked down at my shoes, and slowly scanned my way up.

I had the same legs I always had; the same waist I always had; the same chest I always had. That was a relief. (Freud, Freud, Freud. It's practically textbook.) Then I looked up a little farther and realized that—Oh, no! It's true!—there was an Emilio growing out of my neck.

I resolved then and there to never, never, *never* shave my mustache again. I would guard it with my life, coddle it, nurture it, and keep it free of crumbs, lice, and rodents. (As Adler explained, people strive to attempt an ideal in order to compensate for feelings of helplessness in childhood. And now that I think about it, I desperately wanted a mustache when I was five, but was unable to grow one.)

In order to achieve this ideal, I bought a shaving mirror, an electric mustache trimmer, even a special mustache comb. (As Jung observed, the goal of development is unity within the personality.) And I was safe. Until last Sunday.

Just as I was about to take my shower, I realized that my mustache was bushier than usual, so I took out my electric mustache trimmer and gave myself a buzz.

One, two, three—and I was done. It looked fine.

Once my mustache was trimmed, though, I realized that my hair looked a little bushy, too. And my new, neat mustache made my hair look even worse. The top was kind of spiky. The sides were hanging over my ears. Hmm ... It seemed kind of daring to use a mustache trimmer on my head, but I was just going to take care of a few stray hairs. Should I? Shouldn't it?

Oh, what the heck.

I buzzed the top, buzzed the sides, and waddya know? Nothing to it! Easy as pie. But when I was done, I realized one side seemed more trimmed than the other. So I buzzed some more and waddya know? A big tuft of hair fell into the sink.

Oh, my God.

I took a deep breath, tried not to cry, and told myself, "I can fix this. Nothing to it." So I buzzed, and I buzzed, and I cried a little, and I buzzed and ... (As Erickson noted, failure to successfully resolve a crisis results in fixation.)

If there was a little voice telling me to stop, I didn't hear it over the buzzing. I was a madman. And by the time I was finished, there was hardly anything left. The tops and sides were trimmed down to the nubs. The back—why on earth did I do the back?—looked like little men with razor blades on their feet had been skiing all over my head.

It was such a mess that I ran to my barber on Tuesday morning pleading with him to even it all out. As I shared the gory details, he nodded, knowingly.

"You're my third one today," he said. "This sort of thing is symptomatic of certain stress disorders. But I wouldn't be too concerned about it. As Fromm wrote, 'Spontaneous activity is the one way in which man can overcome the fear of aloneness without sacrificing the integrity of his self.'"

"Really?" I asked if he could put together the shattered mosaic of my sad and tortured existence. (Not to mention the shattered mosaic of my sad and tortured scalp.)

"No problem," he said. "Ten bucks."

A genuine bargain.

The Cat Problem

When I was twelve or so, I developed a nasty case of hay fever. Summers were hell. I'd sneeze so much I'd lose my equilibrium. But people were always understanding and sympathetic. My sneezing fits seemed to bring out the mensch in everybody: "Are you OK? Is there anything I can do? Do you want to lie down? Do you want a pillow? Some water? Chocolate pudding?"

Chocolate pudding?

Shortly after I turned sixteen, the hay fever went away and never came back. There was no explanation except that I had "outgrown" it. Fine with me. But then three years later while visiting a friend, I sneezed for no apparent reason.

Then I sneezed again. Then I started getting itchy—my scalp, my mustache, under my arms ... now what?

"I don't know," my friend Eddie said. "Maybe it's the cat."

The cat?

Over the next three years, the situation worsened. I discovered that whenever I was around a cat, my eyes would water, I'd itch anywhere there was hair on my body, and my eyelids would swell up with huge welts.

I also learned that for some bizarre reason, the less you want to be around a cat, the more a cat wants to be around you.

I hated this even more than I hated the hay fever. Worse, though, was the fact that *no one* was understanding or sympathetic. I'd be sitting in someone's living room—the friend of a friend, the relative of someone I was dating—and then out of nowhere, some feline would stride by, rub her tail on my pants leg, and I'd jump ten feet into the air.

"You have a cat!"

"Yes. Isn't she adorable? And she likes you! She hardly ever goes up to strangers like that."

For reasons I have never quite fathomed, no one wants to believe that you could possibly be allergic to *their* cat:

"You can't be allergic to *my* cat. He's the cleanest cat in the world."

"You can't be allergic to *my* cat. She's just a kitten."

"You can't be allergic to *my* cat. He's Siamese."

Hey, I don't care if he was born in Peru, educated at Oxford, and summers in the Hamptons. Get his little Siamese butt out of my sight.

Allergy medications didn't help. And as the condition worsened, so did the responses I got. Not only were people unsympathetic, but they started apologizing *to the cats.*

"I'm sorry I have to put you in the bathroom, honey-baby, but the big man's afraid of you."

When I was twenty, my girlfriend Donna's ditzy aunt Helen told her tabby, "I have to put you downstairs for a little while, Sheba, because Donna's boyfriend is a little grumpy and doesn't like you." She then turned to me and said, "I don't think Sheba has ever been in an allergic situation before."

I see.

Has Sheba ever been in a microwave?

Two weeks ago, a neighbor invited me to a party some friends were throwing at their house in Hackensack. It sounded like fun. But when I got there, I saw a cat. Then another. Then a third.

Three cats?

I took a deep breath. Through the years, I'd developed a fairly effective coping strategy for surprise "cat-frontations." One is to simply say I'm sorry and leave. The other is to politely request that the cat be put in another room. I then seek out something to sit on that isn't covered in fabric (leather or wood is usually fine) and try to make the best of things.

For a while, this seemed to work. The party was being held in the host's basement, and two of the cats seemed content to stay in an upstairs bedroom.

But the third was a troublemaker. When he came up to me, I whispered "Go away."

When he rubbed up against my leg, I nudged him and hissed. When he climbed onto my lap, I jumped up so quickly he bounced onto the coffee table.

None of this deterred him.

I bolted upstairs. The cat followed. I ran from the living room to the kitchen. The cat followed. I rushed from the kitchen to the bathroom. The cat followed. I ran back into the living room, then the kitchen, then the foyer, then back to the bathroom. *The cat was chasing me around the house.*

In a cold sweat, I ran out of the front door and got into my truck, itching like crazy. In the rearview mirror I could see that my eyes were already swelling up. I drove onto Essex Street, made the turn onto Route 17, and stopped at a light. A long, black sedan pulled up next to me. The cat was driving it.

When the signal changed, I hit the gas so violently I left skid marks. The cat did the same. He chased me down Route 17, up Route 3, down Route 46, and back onto 17, as I tried desperately to lose him.

In Hasbrouck Heights, a cop pulled me over. He walked over to my car carrying a flashlight in one hand and a cat in the other. I screamed.

"Oh, don't tell me you're afraid of cats," the officer said.

No one understands.

Foof Shoes

Two months ago when I went on a spending rampage and bought a bunch of summer clothes—to wear to all those garden parties I never get invited to—I knew, inevitably, that I was going to have to buy some nice new shoes to go along with all my nice new shirts, nice new jackets, and nice new trousers.

I've always been one of those people who says, "This looks fine, I'll take it ..." without really thinking about it, or trying it on, or shopping around.

But recently the problem has intensified to the point where I want to be in and out in fifteen minutes or less.

This usually works OK with with shirts, jackets, and trousers because I can always have them altered or bring them back or give them to someone else for a birthday present. But you can't do this sort of thing with shoes because—*foof, foof*—you can really get burned.

Anyway, I did buy a nice new pair of shoes not too long ago—a nice new, charcoal gray, suede-looking, rubber-soled pair of shoes, to be exact. And I thought they looked pretty cool, and when I tried them on they seemed to fit pretty well, so I told the salesman I'd take them.

"Do you want to walk around in them a bit?" he asked.

And I said, "No, no, they're fine. Just wrap 'em up and charge 'em."

Foof, foof.

Trouble on the way.

The shoes were more than $100 *and* they were on sale, which meant I couldn't return them, but I was so intent on buying them and running home that I didn't pay much attention to that.

Three days later, I got all dressed up to go to dinner, in my nice new shirt, my nice new jacket and my nice new trousers. And, naturally, I put on my nice, new shoes to complete what the men's fashion magazines like to call "a nice new look." I then ran out of the house and drove into New York to pick up my friend Jane. But as we were leaving her apartment building, she stopped suddenly and asked, "What was that?"

I stopped walking and said, "What was what?"

"I don't know," she said. "I heard a *foof*."

"What's a *foof*?"

"You know," she said, "a *foof* sound. Something going *foof*."

We continued walking, and then I heard it too. It was my shoes. My shoes were *foofing*. Making a *foof* sound. *Foofing* like crazy. I was wearing—oh, my God—*foof* shoes.

Jane looked down at my feet. "Are those new?" she asked.

"Yeah," I said. "I bought them a couple of weeks ago. They were more than $100."

She began to laugh. "You spent more than $100 on shoes that *foof*?"

People in the lobby began laughing and pointing. "*Foof* shoes! *Foof* shoes!"

I was so embarassed, I ran out of the building, sat in my truck, and wept.

Passers-by, seeing how upset I was, began pounding on my windows and yelling:

"What's the matter, big guy? Got *foof* shoes?"

People can be so cruel.

Over the next few days, I tried everything: foam insoles ... toilet paper in the heel ... I even twisted the shoes back and forth in my hands, hoping to break them in a little and kill the *foof*. But it didn't do any good. Everywhere I went, I *foofed,* and everytime I *foofed* people would point and whisper and laugh. I was despondent.

My friends tried to be supportive. "It's just a matter of time," they'd say. "The *foof* will go away." But it didn't.

Then one afternoon as I was *foofing* through the drugstore, a young woman came up to me. "You *foof*, don't you?" she asked, gently. "So do I."

We embraced, with tears in our eyes, rocking back and forth, and *foofing* like a house on fire. "You don't have to feel different," she said, handing me a card. "There's a wonderful *foof* bar in Jersey City, where it's OK to *foof*. You can *foof* all night."

"I can? You're kidding me!"

Well, believe it or not, she was right. And, believe it or not, I went, I *foof*ed, I met other *foof*ers, we *foof*ed together. I felt accepted. And I loved it. I went four times a week. I was a *foof*ing fool. But then one night for no apparent reason, the *foof*ing stopped. I was on the dance floor, *foof*ing away, and then all of a sudden, *silence.*

People pointed at me. They whispered. They laughed. How could they do this to me? I thought they were my friends. But they weren't.

"What's the matter, big guy?" someone asked. "Can't *foof* anymore?"

People can be so cruel.

In Search of Barbra

Two months ago, at the stroke of noon, I called Ticketmaster, in search of Barbra Streisand tickets. So did everyone else in the world. It took thirty-five minutes of speed dialing, but I finally got through. And I was rewarded with six seats. In six different sections.

I told the ticket agent I was going with friends. "I'd kind of like to sit with them. How about the other nights?"

The other nights were no better. "We're almost completely sold out," he said.

"OK," I told him, "how about four seats over here and two over there?"

"No good."

"Three and three?"

"No."

"Two, two, and two?"

"No, but don't worry about it," he said. "You've got good seats."

Famous last words: "Don't worry about it" and "You've got good seats."

OK, I didn't worry about it.

And, OK, my seat was good: comfortable, sturdy. It went up and down when I told it to. And it was closer to the stage than, say, Australia is to Puerto Rico. But when you come right down to it, what I had really gotten were five good seats and one lousy one. So guess which member of my party wound up with the lousy one?

Never mind that I got the tickets in the first place.

Never mind that I did all the speed dialing and haggling on the phone while my friends were sleeping, or filing their nails, or lounging by the pool eating bon-bons.

Never mind that all six tickets ($125 each, plus tax, plus service charges, plus mailing costs) went on my Visa card.

When we finally got to the Garden and everyone drew a ticket, I wound up with the clinker. The stinker. The runt of the litter.

And I don't care what anyone tells you: On a clear day, you can't see forever.

My friend Ed—whom I don't even like—was sitting so close to the stage he could have hit the woman with a spitball. Danny was a little farther back, but he was on the floor of the Garden, in one of the $350 seats. Jan and her sister Diane were also down there, poor things. And my friend Scott, who was sitting slightly higher up, was still close enough to have a bird's-eye view of ol' Barb.

He also wound up sitting next to an executive from Sony who took a shining to him and promised to mail him a truckload of CDs.

And then there was me: tower A, gate 60, section Z, seat 6,793. Where is that exactly? I'll tell you: You just have to keep walking—past the burgundy seats, past the blue seats, past the green seats, through the Holland Tunnel ... if I'd walked five more minutes I would have been in Amish country.

During the intermission Ed was nice enough to rub it in. "Did you see the way she arched her eyebrow when she started singing "People"?

You could tell where we were sitting by our responses:

DANNY: You saw her eyebrows?
JAN: You saw her face?
ME: She sang "People"?

When the lights dimmed and the overture began, everyone around me started pulling out opera glasses, binoculars, telescopes, and I was sitting there with absolutely nothing because—you know —I had "good seats."

The next thing I knew, Streisand entered, through a white curtain, onto a white stage, and sat on a white chair. She was wearing a white dress, white shoes, and white stockings.

Did I see her?

No.

It would have been easier to find a grain of salt in a sack of flour.

I don't even think I could have picked her up on radar.

"Oh, here she comes ..." the woman next to me said as she peered through her binoculars. Her name was Laurel.

"Where?" I whispered.

"Over there," Laurel said, pointing.

"Where?"

"There."

"Oh, are you sure?"

"Of course. How can you miss her? Doesn't she look great?"

Within minutes, Laurel was gushing all over the place. She'd seen Barbra in Central Park in 1968 and saw her on New Year's Eve in Las Vegas.

"You really get around," I said.

"Oh, that's what everybody says," she told me. "I was at the ticker-tape parade for the Rangers last week, and I also went to Woodstock, the 1992 Democratic convention, and I was at Shea Stadium the night the Mets won the World Series."

"That's incredible," I told her.

"And guess where I was when Kennedy was assassinated!"

"In the limo?"

"No! I was with my grandmother, shopping in Times Square. And I'll never forget the commotion!"

"That's great, Laurel, but why don't we listen to the—"

"It's history, really, being here. Something you can tell your grandchildren about, just like the moon landing and the—"

"Laurel …"

"Of course, Barbra's my favorite. And seeing her live in New York, with all these people … and you know what they say: People who need people …"

You should have seen the way she arched her eyebrow when I bit her on the leg.

Facing the Inevitable

I have to face facts here: For forty-one, I don't look so good.

At least that's what everybody keeps telling me. And it's been going on for months now.

I'd walk into the office and somebody would say, "Hi. No sleep last night?"

I love that one.

"No, I slept fine. Why?"

"Oh, nothing. You just look ... tired."

My second favorite, generally from other guys: "Hey, hey, hey! You must've had fun last night! You look like hell!"

"No, I didn't have any fun last night, but thanks anyway."

Third favorite: "Are you feeling OK? You look terrible."

All right! OK! I look tired. I look terrible. I look like hell. I get the picture.

Now what?

A few weeks ago I went home and did something rather radical: I took a nice long look in the mirror.

To be perfectly honest with you, I didn't care for it.

I started by taking a good look at my eyes. They were puffy, with thick bags underneath. So I went to the kitchen, got a pencil and paper, and wrote down:

1. Bags under eyes.

Whenever possible, I try to approach these things in an organized, scientific fashion.

I returned to the mirror and also noticed a certain heaviness around my eyelids and the bridge of my nose, almost like a shadow of some kind. I can't quite explain it. It just didn't look right to me.

After a few minutes of turning this way and that, I finally put my fingers on my forehead, pulled the skin up, and everything looked fine again. Hmm ...

1. Bags under eyes.

2. Face collapsing.

There was also a kind of grayness to my skin that bothered me. I have an olive complexion and always look pretty awful in the winter. And it's pretty annoying, especially since other people always look so pink and happy all winter long.

I tried pinching my cheeks to give them a little color, but nothing happened.

So I washed my face vigorously, but nothing happened. So I grabbed some witch hazel and slapped it on, harder, and harder, and *harder*. I must've slapped myself thirty-five times. It was worth it, though. My skin went from a drab, creepy, dark gray to a bright, festive, light gray.

1. *Bags under eyes.*
2. *Face collapsing.*
3. *Gray face.*

I decided there probably wasn't anything I could do about any of these things. But when another friend at work told me how miserable I looked, I knew I had to at least make an attempt.

On the way home from work that day I stopped at the drugstore and kind of, sort of, wandered around the Smelly Stuff for Your Face aisle.

Now I'm not exactly Mr. Macho, but I still have a problem with things like this. I can't pick up something that says "Maybelline" without feeling a burning sensation in my fingers.

Behind the counter was an absolutely gorgeous woman who looked as if she'd just jumped off the cover of *Mademoiselle*. She was giving out samples of some new rejuvenating skin cream. "Would you like to try some?" she inquired. "I've been using it for two months already, and I can't believe the difference!"

"And you are how old?" I asked.

"Eighteen," she said.

We had a little heart to heart.

"Look," I told her, "I don't feel terribly comfortable using stuff like this. But I've been having a few—what would you call them?—facial problems in the last few months. Nothing major, mind you. I doubt you could even tell by looking at me …"

"No, I can tell," she said. "You have bags under your eyes, your skin is gray, your face is collapsing, and the sides of your nose ..."

"All right, Tootsie, let's stop there. So what would you suggest? I mean for *men*. Do you have any *men* stuff? Stuff *manly* men put on their *manly* faces? I don't want anything that smells like pussy willows and I don't want to spend a lot of money."

"No problem," she said.

I arrived home half an hour later—and $115 lighter—with my new Moisture Balance Cleansing Lotion, my Age Smoothing Toner, my Revitalizing Alpha Hydroxy Moisture Whip, my Alpha Hydroxy Creme Facial Treatment, my Eye Defense with Liposomes, my Swisspers Premium Cotton Rounds ("Better than cotton balls!"), and my blue plastic mask filled with goo that you put in the freezer for fifteen minutes and then wear on your face for an hour or two while you're watching the Rangers, the basketball game, or the Martha Stewart special on how to make your own big fluffy slippers.

Oh, this is ridiculous.

I put on the mask, attached the Velcro tabs in the back, and walked over to the mirror. "Stop right there, Penguin! It is I, Plutonium Man!"

I immediately took off the mask and put it back in the freezer. Maybe one of my pork chops can wear it to a party or something.

That out of the way, I washed my face and tried the cleansing, toning, revitalizing regimen. According to instructions, I was supposed to see a "fresh, radiant, younger-looking complexion" in just four weeks. It didn't smell like anything, and actually felt OK, so I decided to give it a shot.

Just three weeks later my friend Steve stopped me in the hall at work. "Wow," he said, "what happened to you?"

I couldn't help but smile. "Are you talking about my fresh, radiant, younger-looking complexion?"

"Very funny," he said. "No, really, you look like hell. Wild time last night?"

"No," I said as I knocked him to the ground and sprayed Age Smoothing Toner in his eyes.

Plutonium Man has had it with the insults.

Shut My Mouth

In the course of an average day I probably spend between fifteen and twenty minutes on my teeth, doing the brushing business, the flossing frightfulness, and the gargling gruesomeness.

In years past I also did the Water-Pic witlessness, which took twenty minutes all by itself. In this once-popular procedure, you would casually slide a hose between your lips and proceed to shoot water into every corner of your mouth—not to mention every corner of your bathroom—until your mouth felt clean and fresh and the mirror on your medicine cabinet looked like a Jackson Pollack.

I'm not going to bore you with the wretched details of my wretched, media-manipulated childhood: "Look, Ma, no cavities!" "Ultra Brite gives your mouth sex appeal!" Et cetera. But there's no escaping the fact that my generation is mouthphobic. Our teeth can never be white enough. Our gums can never be pink enough. Our lips can never be moist enough. And our breath can never be sweet enough.

When someone comes close to us we cringe because we're afraid our mouths won't have that fresh, clean, "natural" smell of mint leaves, pine trees, azalea bushes, or whatever natural thing Listerine is supposed to smell like.

Because of this phobia, trips to the dentist tend to be uncomfortable. There are other reasons, of course, most of them having to do with pain and bloodshed. But more than anything else, we are traumatized by the idea of someone's poking around in there and finding it … well … unsatisfactory.

Half an hour before my appointment last week, I spent at least fifteen minutes brushing, rebrushing, flossing, and gargling. (And I was going in for a cleaning.)

In keeping with the brainwashing I've undergone during the past twenty-five years, I wanted to make a good impression, even though I know from previous experience that no matter how many times I brush, it's never going to be good enough. He (the dentist) or she (the hygienist) is going to march into my mouth with mirrors and probes, make a left at my molars, and find a whole head of broccoli back there.

Then they're going to wave it in my face, which I've come to recognize as another form of psychological torture. "Ooh, what's this?" they'll ask. "Didn't you read that leaflet I gave you on proper flossing methods?"

Last week's appointment—with the hygienist—started off poorly, but I'm not blaming anyone in particular. I had gotten there a little early, picked up the new issue of *Highlights,* and saw that some little brat had already circled everything on the hidden pictures page. For some reason, he also circled everything on Goofus and Gallant, The Timbertoes, and the table of contents.

I was annoyed, but I dealt with it.

When I went in, the hygienist looked over my very satisfactory charts—I had no cavities, in case you're interested—and then looked in my mouth, at which point she started grimacing and turning up her nose like she'd just seen some big greasy rat smoking a cigar.

Just between us, I could use a little stroking now and then. I mean, my major goal growing up was to have as few cavities as possible. Now, as an adult, I don't have any cavities. But instead of putting a little blue star on my chart they pry my mouth open and berate me about plaque.

Plaque this, and plaque that, and plaque, plaque, plaque everywhere you look.

"Look at all that plaque," she instructed in a rather complicated stunt involving two probes, two mirrors, and a headlight from the space shuttle.

I have to admit it looked pretty awful in there. But believe me when I tell you that she was pointing to teeth I had never even seen before. They were like the upper part of the inside of the top molars, all the way in the deepest, darkest corner, somewhere to the right.

"How'd you miss that?" she wanted to know.

"I don't have all this equipment," I told her.

"You don't need any special equipment," she told me as her 2,000-watt overhead light burned out my retinas.

Eventually, it was time to begin the cleaning, which is now officially called a scaling—don't ask me why. It starts with a little buzzing action, then a little abrasion action, and then a little rinse-and-spit action.

"Did that hurt?" she asks.

Trust me when I tell you this: Never say no. When they ask about pain, you should yell, scream, jump up and down, and threaten to call the police. Curse at them. Roll your eyes. Kick their instruments off the console.

Never say no.

Of course, nitwit that I am, I told her I didn't feel a thing. The next thing I knew she threw this pirate hook in my mouth and was sticking it into my gums, waiting until it hooked onto something, and then *yanking* it back out with such force she pulled me right out of the chair. After about fifteen minutes of this hooking and yanking I finally made a noise loud enough for the entire office to hear. And do you know what she said to me?

"Shush!"

Not "What's the matter?"

Not "Are you okay?"

Just "Shush."

I wanted to tell her I'd be glad to stick a pickax down her throat and see how she liked it, but I did nothing of the sort because she still had a sharp object resting on my tongue.

Twenty minutes later when it was all over, she asked me to fill out a little card, sign it, and put the date on it.

"What's this for?" I asked as she washed my blood off the ceiling.

She said the receptionist had a file of these cards and that in six months she would mail it to me as a reminder to come in for another "cleaning."

"What a clever idea," I told her. Then I signed the card—Bill Ervolino—and dated it—April 5, 2037.

Waiting for Dr. Godot

I don't know if any of you are old enough to remember this, but there was a time when you could go into a doctor's examining room and someone would actually stop by and say hello within fifteen or twenty minutes, if only to see if you were still breathing.

Now you spend more time waiting in the examining room than you spend waiting in the waiting room. In fact, you spend more time in the examining room than the person who built the examining room.

It's almost like going to a restaurant and being told that even though you have a reservation, you have to sit at the bar for a while. The only difference is that in the doctor's office you're lying on your back, no one offers you a drink, you feel like throwing up, and most of your clothes are hanging on a doorknob.

Part of the problem is that doctors now have thirty-three examining rooms instead of one, and while you're lying there in a semiconscious state, they're running from room to room like the Marx Brothers.

GROUCHO: Say "aah."
HARPO: Honk!
GROUCHO: Say "aah."
HARPO: Honk!
GROUCHO: Say "aah."
HARPO: Honk!

When the doctor finally does stop by, you have to handcuff him to something or he'll be in your mouth, in your nose, in your ears, and out the door before you know what hit you.

YOU: Doctor, I've been feeling a little …
DOCTOR: I see. OK. Sit up. Turn to the side. Make a fist. Say "aah." Count to ten. Look over there. Look back. Again. Again. Just as I thought. I'm giving you this.

	Take it all. Call me if there's a problem. Bye.
YOU:	But …

Then the nurse comes back and makes some small talk, just so you feel like you got your $75 worth.

NURSE:	That was the new doctor. Doesn't he look just like Richard Gere?
YOU:	(*putting on your clothes*): I guess so. I didn't really get a good look at him.
NURSE:	Well, he is a quick one. I don't know if you noticed, but he removed your tonsils.

Doctors and dentists are busy people, and that's fine by me. They can see ten thousand patients a day for all I care. More power to 'em. But if I have to wait for half an hour, why can't I wait in the waiting room, sitting up, reading a magazine? Why do I have to lie there, on my back, in those little pastel rooms, with the door closed, the curtains drawn, nothing to do, no one to talk to, and nothing to look at but four cabinets, twelve drawers, and a plastic skeleton?

Well, hello there, Mr. Skeleton. And how long have you been waiting?

On the few occasions that I've complained about this system to the nurse, I've received answers I didn't care for:

1. "I'm sorry, but it's been a horrible day." (Is that an original line or what? I haven't heard anyone say they were having a nice day since 1973.)
2. "It's faster this way. The doctor's time is very valuable." (Yeah? Well, what about my time? I'm a busy professional too, you know. The least you could do is give me a few comic books and a lollipop.)
3. "We do this so people have time to disrobe." (The only people who need half an hour to disrobe are arthritics, asthmatics, and scuba divers. Besides, I'm a man. I can have all my clothes on the floor in fifteen seconds.)

Of course, I could go on and on till the cows come home, but it wouldn't make any difference. So rather than complain, I've come up with a few fun things to do while waiting in an examining room. Try them the next time you're sitting around with nothing else to do:

1   Open all the drawers and rearrange their contents in interesting new ways.
2.   Glue the tongue depressors together into Oriental serving trays and sell them to other patients.
3.   Scream something about rats.
4.   Loosen all the screws on the X-ray machine.
5.   Sit on top of the X-ray machine and pretend it's your old friend Barney the dinosaur.
6.   Point the X-ray machine out the window and blast passers-by with excessive amounts of radiation.
7.   Unroll all of the paper on the examining table and crumple it into a large ball. (Later, when the doctor asks what it is, tell him you coughed it up.)
8.   Draw a bull's-eye on the door and hurl syringes at it.
9.   Try to pull off all the wallpaper without disturbing any of the diplomas.
10.   Call Domino's every five minutes, give them the address, and say "Send three more with anchovies."

The Fan

Like many gentlemen of a certain age, I'm pretty much set in my ways. I want all my shirts to be hanging in the same direction. I want to eat dinner at around 9 P.M. And I want fans to be on at all times. You know what a fan is, don't you? It's this thing. You plug it in the wall. You turn it on. It blows air around.

But more on that later.

Like many people who live in apartment complexes, I have no control whatsoever over the heat that comes pouring through my baseboards. Some people never get enough heat. Some, like me, are bombarded with it from October to April, no matter what the temperature is outside, no matter how often we complain.

Through the years, I've gotten used to having fans on, all year-round, to keep my apartment at a certain temperature, to keep fresh air circulating, and to make sure that my neighbors never stop by, start sniffing around, and tell me that my home smells like cigars, dirty socks, or the sausage and pepper stand at the San Gennaro festival.

Is this so weird?

Plus, I've gotten so used to the hum, I have trouble sleeping unless there's a fan whirring nearby.

As a result, I tend to go through several fans in the course of a year. In the summer when one of them conks out on me, I just go to a store and replace it.

But in nonsummer months I go through hell.

My local five-and-ten relegates fans to their "seasonal" department. By mid-August this seasonal junk (which includes lawn chairs and hibachis) is consolidated into a slightly smaller department, which keeps mysteriously shrinking and shrinking until three minutes after Labor Day, when it all just disappears off the face of the earth.

In September, when I asked if they had any fans in stock, the manager told me no.

"That's seasonal," he said.

"I understand that," I told him. "But I thought perhaps you had some in the back somewhere."

He insisted he didn't.

"Downstairs? Upstairs? In a warehouse on the outskirts of town? I don't mind driving. I could knock on the back door. Say 'Joe sent me ...'"

"No."

"But I don't understand. Three weeks ago you had about twenty of them right over there, where the Christmas trees are."

"Well, we don't have any more," he said. "It's September. People don't buy fans in September."

No. They buy Christmas trees.

I left there and went to a housewares store. Same thing. This time I spoke to a woman who was sitting behind a counter. To her left was a tiny electric fan that was blowing in her face.

"It's September," she told me. "What do you need a fan for?"

Resigned to the fact that I wasn't going to find a new fan—because someone, somewhere has decided I didn't need or want one—I began moving the ones that still worked from room to room.

In November, a second fan started acting up. It was making a loud shrieking noise. And when I got closer I smelled something burning. So I turned it off, pulled out the plug, and tossed it in the trash.

And then there was one.

I went to more stores, where I was told, "It's November. What do you want a fan for?"

"I slice salami with it."

I mean, come on. How many things does a fan do? You plug it in. You turn it on. It blows air around.

Carvel is open all year long!

My grocery store sells genetically altered watermelons in February!

Why can't I get a fan?

I'll pay extra! I'll special order! I'll fly to Tokyo to pick it up!

What do I have to do?

Tell me!

Now here it is January. Over the weekend, as the temperature outside hovered around 60 and the heat in my apartment hovered around 120, I sat down with the Yellow Pages and called every appliance store in the fair State of New Jersey.

One woman just repeated everything I said: "You want a fan? You keep fans on all the time? It blows air around? I don't understand ..."

I eventually called one of those giant appliance warehouses, where there are always seven hundred manic employees running around like they're on the floor of the New York Stock Exchange. "You want a TV? I'll give you a deal! You want a VCR? I'll give you a deal! You want a Walkman? A Discman? A Pac-Man? A Game Boy? A Lay-Z-Boy? Tell me what you want!"

A woman answered the phone. I told her I wanted a fan. She asked what kind of fan. I said, "A fan fan. An electric fan. You plug it in. You turn it on. It blows air around."

She asked if I meant that I wanted an exhaust fan.

I told her no.

She asked if I meant that I wanted a fan heater.

I told her no.

She asked if I meant that I wanted a ceiling fan.

"What is the *matter* with you people? I just want a *fan*! A plain electric *fan*! You plug it *in*! You turn it *on*! Where *are* they? What have you *done* with them?"

She took a deep breath and said, "Sir, it's January. What do you want a fan for?"

Oh, who the hell knows? I don't even remember anymore.

High and Dry

It doesn't take a whole hell of a lot to throw my sad, little life into turmoil.

On Tuesday morning on my way to work, I drove to my neighborhood laundromat. I've been doing this, every other week, for almost seven years now. I drop off my clothes, sheets, and towels in the morning. And I pick them up, washed, folded, and pressed in the afternoon.

For someone who's never been able to learn the finer points of cold, warm, and hot, and who couldn't fold a contour sheet if you held a staple gun to his head, this has always been a wonderful, wonderful thing.

Better than candy bars.

But on Tuesday, my candy bar melted.

At first, I didn't know what was going on. When I drove into the parking lot, I was surprised (and happy) to see that there wasn't a single car in the lot. Zip. Zero. Nada.

Great.

I can't tell you how inconvenient it is to haul my big bag of laundry past all those inconsiderate people who insist on washing, drying, and folding their own laundry, and blocking the aisles, with bags, carts, and so forth, while their adorable little children run around screaming, jumping, kicking, yelling, screaming, playing tag, banging on the windows, screaming, screaming, making noise, and screaming.

Why are children always screaming?

And why do they always have to scream louder than the noise level of wherever they happen to be? Can't they scream softly, to themselves, instead of acting like spoiled, rotten, out-of-control brats?

Anyway, I got to the front door of the laundromat—dragging my big, black nylon bag filled with clothes, towels, and sheets—grasped the door handle firmly with my left hand, and pulled.

Nothing.

So I pulled again.

Nothing.

Hmm … the door is locked.

Why is the door locked?

I pushed my face up to the big glass door and looked inside, hoping to see the warm friendly face of my dear, beloved laundress.

Nothing.

No face. No laundress. No laundromat.

It was gone.

Not closed. Not on vacation. Not "No one's here, be back in ten minutes."

It was gone.

The front desk was gone.

The little laundry carts were gone.

The washing machines were gone.

All I saw was this center island where the washing machines *used* to be, with a bunch of pipes coming up from the floor—leading nowhere—and a bunch of metal knobs standing around doing nothing.

Despite this, I actually tried opening the *other* door, as if the other door would lead me into a fully functioning, fully equipped laundromat, which, of course, it fully didn't.

Why do I do stuff like this? Last week, I opened my refrigerator door seventeen times looking for a strawberry yogurt. I moved things around, closed the door, walked away, went back, opened the door, moved things around, walked away, came back, moved things around, went away, came back, went away …

So there I was, standing on the street with my big, black nylon bag. People were strolling by. Cars were zooming past. And I just stood there.

It was a bit like waking up, walking to the bathroom, and finding that someone had bricked it up during the night.

Anything would have helped. An out-of-business sign. A remodeling sign. A we-were-robbed sign. A for-sale sign.

How could they leave me high, dry, *and* signless? I'm a single man! I don't know how to do laundry! I can't fold! I can't press! *What have you done to me?*

And I've been going there for seven years! Couldn't they have warned me? Said something? Dropped hints? ("Do you know what Clorox is? Buy some.")

OK—deep breath, deep breath—enough of that. I trudged back to the car and considered my options: Find another laundromat that washes, folds, and presses; do it myself; drive to my mother's house; marry.

I stared intently at passers-by.

I'll cook, vacuum, and *clean the bathroom if you'll do the laundry.*

No takers.

So I went to work, sat through a meeting (whimpering), returned to my desk, made some calls.

"Hi. Do you wash, fold, and press?"

"No."

"Then what the hell good are you?"

My boss, sensing my delicate emotional state, sent me home early. "Thanks," I said. "I'll be better tomorrow." (I'll be in dirty, wrinkled clothes, but I'll be better.)

Back at my apartment, I found a card in the mailbox: "Thinking of you on the loss of your laundromat."

That was sweet. Friends are so important at times like this.

Feeling alone, empty, dejected, and lost, I trudged up the steps with my big, black nylon bag and searched through some sale fliers for Clorox coupons.

Life does go on, doesn't it? We have to be resourceful, strong, brave, and mature ... don't we?

Of course, we do.

Finding a suitable coupon, I drove to the A&P and asked for directions to the Clorox aisle, where I found other single, suddenly laundromatless men like me.

We spent the next ten minutes screaming, jumping, kicking, yelling, screaming, playing tag, banging on the windows, screaming, screaming, making noise, and screaming.

Hey, one day at a time ...

Watching My Back

The worst thing about having excruciating back pain is that you generally don't look as though anything is wrong with you.

The second worst thing about having excruciating back pain is that the people around you *don't* have excruciating back pain.

They see you at work, or call you on the phone, or stop by to visit, and they're always saying stupid things like "Hi! What's new?"

And you sneer at them and say, "I'm in excruciating back pain."

And they say, "Oh, that's terrible. Do you want to go to a movie or something?"

And you say, "No, I don't want to go to a movie or something. I'm in pain."

And they say, "Do you want to get something to eat?"

And you say, "No, I don't want to get something to eat. I'm in pain."

And they say, "Do you want to...?"

And you say, "*No!* I don't want to do anything! I'm in pain! Miserable, horrible, excruciating pain! Have you ever had pain? Do you know what pain is?"

It all started last Saturday when I reached down under the sink to get my Ivory liquid and screamed so loudly that people in North Vietnam looked out their windows and said, "What was that?"

By Saturday night, my body had become a giant *S*.

By Sunday morning, I looked perfectly fine, but I could barely move. So do you think I got any sympathy? *Noooooooo.*

I called my neighbor across the street, told him I was paralyzed, and asked if he had any muscle relaxers. He said, "Sure. Come and get them."

"Well," I said, "it's really hard for me to walk right now." (Hint, hint …)

He said, "No problem. I'll be home all day."

Thanks.

Honestly, it isn't fair. You break your leg and people fawn all over you. A little open heart surgery and people treat you like a king. But back pain, forget about it. People who've never had it think you're making it up.

"How's your back feeling today? Any better?"

"No. I'm in excruciating pain."

"Oh, that's terrible. I had a mosquito bite on my back last summer. Talk about excruciating! It drove me crazy."

Good. This summer, I hope you get three hundred more.

If they're not trying to outdo you in the pain department, they will do anything to convince you that you're fine.

"You look so rested."

Of course I look rested. I've been lying on my living-room floor for three days, *unable to move*.

This "rested" comment, incidentally, came from my friend Bobby, whom I once saved from choking to death by performing the Heimlich maneuver on him in a restaurant while he was gagging on a piece of steak. And I'm telling you right now: The next time he starts choking on his dinner, I'm going to tell him how rested he looks and ask him to pass the ketchup.

If people aren't trying to convince you that you're fine, they'll ask you precisely what's wrong but won't pay any attention to anything you tell them.

"My lower disk is disintegrating, and when it moves out of alignment all of the nerves become …"

"I'm sorry. Do you have any chips? I'm starving."

"In the kitchen. Anyway, all of the nerves become pinched and it sends shooting pains …"

"Which cabinet? Go ahead. I'm listening."

"Over the microwave. And it sends shooting pains down into your legs and up into your …"

"Tostitos? Great! They're my favorite."

"Down your legs and into your shimmy shimmy koko bop. And it's really painful."

"Gee, that sounds terrible. You wanna watch some TV?"

Even worse than the people who don't listen to you are the ones who do and then offer some idiotic home remedy that worked for the friend of a friend of someone they met on the subway on the way to a Springsteen concert: "I know this is going to sound silly, but someone once told me that if you stand in a doorway, grab on to the molding, lift up your legs, and hang there for about forty-five minutes, your spine will gradually straighten itself out."

"Thanks," I said, looking for a baseball bat. "Of course, I wouldn't have this problem if I could lie down on an escalator once a week. That's what all the big athletes do, you know. Those metal steps slamming into your back are supposed to be the best thing for you. Save you from a life of misery."

"Really? I have to try that sometime."

Oh, please do.

Bald Like Me

It started when I was twenty. I was walking across a parking lot on my way to a delicatessen, when I passed some teenagers playing handball. Just as I was about to exit the lot, the ball rolled by my feet and the kids yelled, "Mister! Could you get the ball?"

Mister?

It was a moment I had been dreading my entire unadult life. A group of teenagers, who couldn't have been more than three years younger than I was, had called me Mister.

Mister.

The party was over, and I knew it was my scalp that had crashed it. I was young. I was thin. I was reasonably attractive. But I was going bald.

I always hated that word.

Bald.

Baldness.

Balding.

Yucch.

Going bald in the Age of Aquarius hadn't been part of my game plan. Hair was everything in those days. And I took such good care of mine. I washed it every day. I used a conditioner. I had a hot comb. I even used Herbal Essence so my head would smell like a garden of earthly delights. But, suddenly, my garden was defoliating. Why was God doing this to me?

At the time, my bald spot was only about the size of a quarter, but it didn't make any difference. I'd see two people whispering and I knew what they were saying: "Honey, look at that little bald man over there."

I was inconsolable.

In an effort to take control of the situation, I went to see a doctor. I felt like an idiot sitting for half an hour in a waiting room filled with people who were coughing, bleeding, and gasping for breath just so I could inquire about my bald spot. But I was desperate.

The doctor was an understanding chap. He asked how old I was.

"Twenty," I told him. "Twenty-one in July."

He smiled at that and shook his head. "Don't you know what happens every seven years?" he asked.

I didn't know what he was talking about. "Every seven years? I don't know. Halley's comet goes by? The Moody Blues have a hit record?"

"No, no, no," he said. "Your body changes. In a couple of months, you'll be twenty-one, so your body is changing."

"Changing into what?"

"Just changing," he told me. "Don't worry about it. Your hair will grow back. These things happen in cycles."

In the meantime, he added, I should try not to wash it so much. Plus I should brush it vigorously twice a day and try changing my part from side to side every couple of months.

"For a change of pace," he said, "part it on the right and let the hair fall on the left."

"I already tried that," I told him. "I parted it on the right and it fell on the floor."

"Have you tried brushing vigorously?"

I showed him the stitches.

"Hmm. Well, keep your shampooing to a minimum, massage your scalp, stand on your head for an hour a day, take vitamins, eat furry animals, don't wear hats, stay out of the sun, cross at the green, not in between, call your mother twice a day, and before you go to bed at night envision yourself with a full head of hair."

Hmm …

None of what he told me made any sense, but I clung to the cycle theory anyway because I had nothing else to hold onto.

My comb had nothing to hold on to, either.

Seven years later, my bald spot had spread across the back of my head like a brushfire. Further complicating matters was that my hairline had begun to recede, so I was getting it from both directions. I knew it was time for a second opinion.

My new doctor provided new words of wisdom. "You're going bald," he told me. "Will that be cash or check?"

Ever calm under pressure, I screamed out like a wounded ante-
lope. "That's it? That's all you can tell me?"

Looking down at my chart he asked me a few questions. "Tell me
about your mother's side of the family," he said. "Your grandfather?"

Bald.

"Uncles?"

Bald.

"Great-uncles? Cousins?"

Bald, bald, bald. "The whole damned family is bald," I sobbed.
"Even the women are bald. The kids. The dogs. The cats. The para-
keets. They're a bunch of cue balls, the whole bleeping, bloody bunch
of them."

"There, there," he said, rubbing my head for luck. "And I suppose
your brother's hair is thinning too."

Suddenly I looked up, a sneer crossing my face. "Thinning? Are
you kidding?

My brother has hair like a gorilla. Mats of it. He has more hair on
his nose than I have on my entire head."

Sob, sob, sob.

"Now stop that crying," he told me, shoving a lollipop into my
mouth. It made me feel a little better until I looked across the room
and saw Telly Savalas in the mirror.

"What you're dealing with," the doctor continued, "is called male
pattern baldness. It's very common and, unfortunately, there's nothing we can do about it."

"Nothing?" I wailed. "C'mon, Doc. There has to be something."

"Well," he said, "I could give you the female hormone estrogen.
That will grow hair, but it has side effects."

"I don't care," I told him. "Just do it."

"You'll grow breasts," he told me.

"How many?"

"Two."

"Where?"

"On your chest."

I mulled it over. "Maybe that's not the best thing for me," I finally
decided. "What else can we do?"

"There is something new," he said. "It's called Minoxodil. But it's expensive, and we don't know for sure if it works. You put it on your scalp twice a day and ..."

I listened carefully and asked him to give me a prescription. Then I left, picked some up, and ran home to get started.

The Minoxodil regimen was simple enough. It came in a bottle with a spongy tip. All you had to do was turn the bottle upside down, wet the sponge, and then dab it on your head. If you did this once in the morning and once at night, the instructions said, you'd probably see new hair growth in about thirty days.

So I did it.

The first time was a little strange. I dabbed a little here, and I dabbed a little there and then stood in front of the mirror and watched a big drop of it slide down my forehead and into my right eye.

The next morning I went back in front of the mirror, redabbed, and watched another big drop slide down my forehead and into my left eye.

After thirty days of this I had some peach fuzz growing on my scalp and eyelashes like Miss Piggy.

People started commenting on the fuzz, but I wasn't particularly impressed. In fact, after all the dabbing and blotting and shaking and fussing I'd just about had it.

The stuff was $89 a bottle, a pain in the neck to use, and I had no idea what it was going to do to me over time. Besides, I asked myself, what's this big deal about hair anyway?

From day one, all I had ever wanted to do was to take control of the situation—so I threw the bottle in the garbage. It was a great feeling. The fuzz eventually fell out, but I didn't care about that, either. And I still don't.

And that's all I want to say on the matter, except for this other piece of good news: My brother, the gorilla, is losing his hair now too. He called a couple of weeks ago to say his sides are thinning, his hairline is receding, and his bald spot widening.

"What can I do about it?" he asked frantically.

Hey, don't come crying to me ... *mister.*

You Had to Be There

I was out for lunch with some guys from work and I heard this joke. It went something like this:

A senior citizen couple go out for a stroll and run into one of their neighbors, a young man who lives a few houses away. The neighbor asks the couple what they've been up to, and the husband says that he and his wife went to a really good restaurant.

The neighbor asks the name of the restaurant, but the older man can't remember. He scratches his head and asks his neighbor, "What's the name of that flower? The one with the thorns on it?"

The neighbor says, "Rose?" And the older man says, "That's it!" Then he turns to his wife and says, "Rose, what was the name of that restaurant we went to?"

I told the joke to a couple of friends and they all seemed to think it was cute. So I thought it might be fun to call my parents and tell it to them. I called the house and my mother answered the phone.

"I have a joke for you," I said.

"Really?" She seemed all excited. "Let me sit down," she said. "OK, go ahead."

So I started telling her the joke:

ME: A senior citizen couple go out for a stroll and run into one of their neighbors, a young man …

HER: Wait, wait … who's this now?"

ME: Who's who?

HER: Who do they run into?

ME: A neighbor, a young man who lives a few houses away. So the neighbor asks the couple what they've been up to, and the husband says that he and his wife went to a really good restaurant. So the neighbor … what's that clicking noise?

HER: Oh, the call waiting. Hold on. (*click*) Hello?

ME: No, it's still me ... try again.

HER: (*click*) Hello?

ME: It's still me. You must've lost them.

HER: (*click*) Hello? Hello?

ME: *Ma, you lost them!* Forget it! (*Deep breath.*) So the neighbor asks what the name of the restaurant was, but the older man can't remember. He scratches his head and asks his neighbor, "What's the name of that flower? The one with the thorns on it?"

HER: Who said this now?

ME: *The old man!* The old man says, "What's the name of the flower? The one with the thorns on it?" And the neighbor says "Rose?"

HER: (*laughing hysterically*) That's so funny!

ME: Ma, that's *not* the end of the joke! The neighbor says, "Rose?" And the older man says, "That's it!" Then he turns to his wife and says, "Rose, what was the name of that restaurant we went to?"

HER: (*laughing*) Oh, that's great. Very funny. As soon as I get off I'll tell your father.

ME: Are you sure you're going to remember it? Tell it back to me.

HER: All right. This couple goes out for a stroll in the park ...

ME: What park? Who said anything about a park? And say, "A couple of senior citizens ..."

HER: A couple of senior citizens go for a stroll in the park and they meet a friend, and they tell him they like to eat at this restaurant but they can't remember the name of it.

ME: Ma, you're ruining it. They went to this restaurant but can't remember the name of it."

HER: Well, that's what I said ... they can't remember the name of it, and the husband says to the friend, "It's the same as the flower with the thorn in it ..."

ME: Ma, you're missing the point here.

HER: I have to tell this to your cousin Rose. She'll really get a kick out of it.

ME: Ma, you're not listening to me. Put Dad on and let me tell the joke to him.

HER: That's probably a better idea. He remembers these things better than I do. Hold on a second. *Emilio! Pick up the extension! Billy's got a joke!*

HIM: Hello? You got a joke? Let's hear it.

ME: OK, these two senior citizens take a stroll and run into this neighbor, a younger man who lives a few houses away …

HER: They were in the park, taking a stroll …

ME: The park … the city dump … *Who cares?* So the younger man asks them what's new and the old man tells him …

HER: Listen to this. It's so funny.

ME: *Ma!* Will you *please* let me finish? And the old man tells him that they went to this great new place to eat, and …"

HIM: (*laughing*) Is this, "Rose, what was the name of that restaurant?"

ME: Yeah …

HIM: That's a good one. Very funny."

ME: Thanks."

As God is my witness, I'm never calling them again.

The Sports Café

Saturday night started off with one of those dead-end, *Marty*esque conversations:

"What do you want to do?"

"I don't know. What do you want to do?"

"I don't know."

I'd spent the day running a zillion errands and had made tentative plans to meet some friends in New York for a little holiday weekend beer guzzling.

But I was tired, and my legs hurt, and I found myself uttering those fateful words: I'm getting too old for this.

As the sun began to set, that's all I was able to think about.

BILL: Do you really want to drive into the city and run around the bars like some dumb kid who has nothing else to do?

BILL: No, I don't.

So I called my friend Fred—one of the few stable people I know—and asked him what he was up to.

"Nothing I can't get out of," he said.

"Same here," I told him. "How about a nice quiet dinner?"

"Sure. What do you feel like eating?"

"I don't know. What do you feel like eating?"

"I don't know. How about ribs?"

"I just had ribs yesterday. How about Italian?"

"Italian's OK. You want Italian?"

"I don't know. What do you want?"

We went to some little Italian place near his house, and I ate like a pig. Well, why not? It was a holiday weekend, and I had nothing else planned. Why not have a good meal?

We left the restaurant a little before 11 and headed back to Fred's house so I could pick up my truck. At least I thought we were heading back to Fred's house.

Actually, all he did was drive a few blocks and park his 4x4 in front of some sports café.

"You're gonna love this place," he told me.

"I am?"

As we approached the door, four college kids jogged past us and were proofed into the bar.

"They proof *everybody* here," Fred told me.

So, naturally, they didn't proof me. In fact, when I reached for my driver's license the doorman winced and said, "What are you, kidding?"

Somebody *please* get me out of here.

"Well, what do you think?" Fred asked as we wended our way to the bar. There was a band onstage playing golden oldies from a hundred years ago—you know: the eighties—and the music was so loud, my fillings were flying out of my mouth.

There were kids dancing. Kids playing pool. Kids hanging around by the speakers. (Are they *totally* deaf?)

As we walked across the dance floor, I realized my big bald head was reflecting the lights like a disco ball.

At the bar, we wedged our way between two kids in tank tops who were smoking Marlboros and watching women in bikinis doing somersaults on ESPN. (Well, after all, this *is* a sports café.)

They saw me walking toward them, noticed the gray in my beard, and moved out of the way so I could get to the bar without tipping over and breaking my hip.

Fred and I both ordered beers. A kid to my left ordered some bright green melon liqueur spritzer in a milkshake glass.

I tried to think of the whole thing as some bold anthropological experiment, but the longer I stood there, the older I felt.

"Don't be silly," Fred told me. "We fit in just fine. How much you wanna bet someone comes up and asks us what school we go to?"

The man is totally hallucinating.

About ten minutes later, though, this perky young co-ed in a halter top walked toward me with a big smile on her face.

I straightened my back, held in my gut, and tilted my head back to relax my wrinkles.

"Hi," she said. "Are you the owner?"

I was going to sit in the bathroom and cry for a while, but the line was too long and my legs were killing me.

Television

Food for Days

On Sunday morning, still bleary-eyed, I made myself some coffee and flicked on the TV just to make sure the world hadn't gone up in flames while I was alseep. I surfed around the dial for a few minutes and then realized—What's this?—I had some *new* channels.

Always a happy day at my house.

I grabbed my cable guide from the coffee table and opened it up to see precisely what had been added.

Hey! Waddya know? I have The Learning Channel!

Hey! Holy smokes! I have Comedy Central!

Hey! *(Oh, no!)* I've got the TV Food Network!

Hmm ... twenty-four hours of people cooking? How could they do this to me?

I purposely go out on Saturday afternoons so I don't have to watch all those food shows on PBS. I don't know why, but I can't keep my eyes off them. And they make me hungry. The guy with the beard cooks soup; I cook soup. The guy with the accent prepares pasta; I prepare pasta. The woman whose hair keeps falling in her face whips up a meringue and ... well, I eat a jelly donut. (Close enough. It's Saturday. I can't spend an hour beating egg whites just so I can have one slice of pie.)

As ridiculous as this is going to sound, I spent the rest of the day (and night) watching my new food channel ... and eating myself into a stupor.

I saw Jacques Pépin making chicken breasts! (And I ate.)

I saw Nathalie Dupree making desserts! (And I ate.)

I saw this man and woman tasting wines and—at least temporarily—lost my appetite. They stuck their noses in each glass, took a quick slug, and smooshed it around in their mouths. He liked most of what he tried and swallowed them.

She hated all of them and spit them out. The camera would pull away to a tight shot of the label, but I could still hear her spitting into a bucket. On national television.

Fabulous.

How'd you like to sit next to her at a dinner party?

But the true highlight of my day came on Sunday evening with Julia Child and Graham Kerr, back to back.

Julia—God love her—was chopping up a goose with a succession of knives that kept getting bigger and nastier. She pulled out some hedge clippers that she used to rip through the rib cage, and then unveiled the final knife of the night—she could have filleted a rhinoceros with this one—placed it on the breast section and started pounding it with a hammer.

Wham! Wham! Wham!

I'm telling you, I was exhausted.

It finally occurred to me that Julia looked awfully young on this show. (Come to think of it, on her most recent PBS series, *Master Chefs,* Julia didn't cook at all. She just had other chefs making their specialties while she tottered around, leaned on the counter, and tried not to fall into the sink.)

Sure enough, this was Julia circa 1970. And if her appearance wasn't enough to give it away, her recipe was. "This is rendered goose fat," she said, pouring a pot of it over the meat.

Good grief.

Then she fried up some onions in pork fat—"In Alsace," she explained, "they use a great deal of lard and onions"—and then started greasing a pan with about three pounds of butter.

Somebody call an ambulance.

All of this was followed by the health-conscious Graham Kerr, on location in New Zealand, making venison with fresh pear juice, leeks, carrots, and juniper berries while I sat on the couch smearing English muffins with peanut butter because—darn it—I was all out of juniper berries.

Don't you hate it when that happens?

"There are a lot of deer in New Zealand," Kerr noted at the top of the show.

Yes, and today we're going to eat one.

Kerr cooks with almost no fat, low sodium, dealcoholized wine … and he prepares things you wouldn't make in a million years.

Fresh pear juice? "It's no problem," he explained. "All you have to do is peel the pears, cut them in half, core them, boil them in a small amount of water, and then remove the halves, retain the liquid, and …"

Graham, go jump in a lake.

For dessert he whipped up some sort of bread pudding that he covered with ice cream made out of soy—Are you listening, Tom Carvel?—and then proceeded to submerge it all in pureed apricots with more dealcoholized wine, bragging as he went: "No sugar! No fat! No alcohol! Times have changed!"

In Alsace, they'd hang him from a tree.

Home Sick

In the pandemonium leading up to (and immediately following) the holidays, I generally find myself telling sneezing, coughing, swollen co-workers to go home where they belong and take their rotten germs, phlegm, and bacterial infections with them.

"Go home! Go to bed! Relax!"

"No, no. I'm fine. *Cough, cough, cough.* Really I am. *Hack, hack, hack.* Thanks anyway. *Sneeze, sneeze, sneeze.*"

Their behavior always confounds me because in the back of my mind I am forever nurturing this benign fantasy of an "out sick" vacation. In it, I am propped up all day on fluffy pillows, drinking herbal tea, nibbling biscuits smeared with apricot jam, reading all that Proust I've been putting off, and listening to Mozart's Concerto for Piano and Orchestra, No. 23 in A major.

Outside my window I see snow swirling above the pavement and people plodding off to work while I gather my robe securely around me and return to my big, comfy bed before my little tootsies get cold.

Of course, when I actually *do* get sick, I realize I don't own any fluffy pillows and proceed to spend my endless, miserable days moaning and groaning, sipping Lipton, reading the instructions that came with my antibiotics, and watching *Maury.*

My nose is red, my tongue looks like *The Bridge on River Kwai,* and my robe … I don't have a robe. But if I did I'm sure it would probably be in the laundry bag or rolled up in a ball in a corner somewhere.

I don't want to be sick anymore. I want to be better. I want to go back to work!

My night table turns into a sad-looking skyline of cups, glasses and pill bottles; my sink overflows with pots, pans, and dishes; and my myriad friends and relatives call periodically—usually just as I'm beginning to nod off—to see if there's anything I need.

"Yes, I need you to get over here, wash my dishes, clean my room, spray everything I own with Lysol, and then go to the store and buy me lots and lots of goodies so I'll have something to look forward to if and when my glands ever shrink back to human size. And, oh yes, bring some fluffy pillows."

I have about twenty books I've been looking forward to reading, if only I had the time. Now I have the time, and I can't even bring myself to read the dustcovers. I don't want to read. I don't feel good!

There were people I wanted to call. Letters I wanted to write. Movies I've been videotaping for the last ten years that I've been hoping to watch. I have hundreds of movies, and I don't want to watch any of them. I don't feel good!

Television, which I've grown to despise because it demands absolutely nothing of me, becomes a bit more attractive—because it demands absolutely nothing of me.

On *Maury* a teenage boy is explaining why he doesn't want to marry his girlfriend who, the boy admits, he has just made pregnant for the *second* time. When someone from the audience asks him a question he says, "My personal life is none of your business," as if they all came to the studio to hear his views on Bosnia.

Of my thirty-seven or so channels, half are devoted to talk shows and soap operas featuring families yelling at each other, and the other half are devoted to shows on home repairs, crafts, and other things people can do with their families when they aren't yelling at each other.

On the Discovery channel I discover a woman who is crinkling up green pieces of paper and gluing them to a Styrofoam ball. When she's done it looks just like a head of cabbage, which, as she explains, "makes a lovely centerpiece."

(Really? In what insane asylum?)

You know this is the kind of mom who can spend hours making paper cabbages and then feed her kids hot dogs and Spaghetti-O's because she's had *such a busy day!*

I hope they're keeping a seat warm for her on *Maury.*

Over on Lifetime, a retired couple is making a shelf.

Together.

Oy.

As the Mrs. explains, she saw this "exact same" shelf in a catalog and loved it, but it cost $60, so she decided to make it herself. With her husband.

The Mr. explains that it's very easy to make. All you need are a few of these doodads from the hardware store, and a few pieces of wood from the lumberyard, and a miter box, and a glue gun, and a work-table, and a can of paint. The whole thing takes only about fifteen hours and costs $445 but, as the Mrs. explains, "It's something you can do together."

If you locked my parents in a room with two hammers, four pieces of lumber, and a glue gun, they'd wind up on the six o'clock news.

When the shelf is finished, the Mrs. paints it cobalt blue—Why, God?—and then hangs it up and puts five pine cones on top of it, so it looks like something you might see in some very neat squirrel's apartment.

Maybe if she has time next week she'll make another shelf for her walnuts.

I turn off the TV, heat up some more tea, and try not to look at myself in a mirror lest I remind myself what a pitiful mess I am.

For the last three months I have dreamed, over and over again, of having a few days to myself to do absolutely, positively nothing.

An hour would have been plenty.

Vas Wasteland

Well here I am, on the couch again, staring at the screen, flicking through the channels, wishing I had a big bag of Tootsie Rolls.

Anything on the ol' tube today?

Hmm ... howzabout some *Gilligan*?

Nah.

Cooking?

Nah.

Old movie?

Nah. Nah. Nah.

How about ...? Hmm ... what *is* that?

I'm sitting on the couch, staring at the screen, wishing I had a big bag of Tootsie Rolls, and looking at what appears to be ...

No, it couldn't be *that*. I mean, they wouldn't show *that* on television. I mean ... well ... they *couldn't*.

Could they?

Eventually, the camera pulls back and I realize, yes, I am looking at a man's ... uh ... how shall I put this?

Oh, to hell with it: I'm sitting on my couch, staring at the screen, watching a man get a vasectomy.

Cancel those Tootsie Rolls.

The man is lying on a table. He has a washcloth over his face. And his entire body is covered with a sheet.

Well, not his *entire* body.

Is this a real person or an actor? ("Johnny, it's your agent! And have I got a part for you!")

Just then, my phone rings. A friend asks what I'm doing. I tell him I'm squirming on my couch, watching a man get a vasectomy. The friend asks why.

Eyes still glued to the—*ouch!*—screen, I tell him—*eek!*—I don't know, as I continue staring—*ooh!*—at this entire operation, moaning and writhing in agony.

"I was just sitting here, flicking through the—*Oh, my God*—channels, and—*Ahh ... I'm getting sick*—I saw this extreme close-up of—

I can't watch this—something that looked vaguely familiar and—*How can they show this on television?"*

My friend wants to know what station I have on. I tell him it's The Learning Channel. He asks if I'm learning anything. I tell him yes, I'm learning that I never want a vasectomy.

He tells me that the week before, he saw someone on TV getting open heart surgery. "It was great," he insisted. "I really learned a lot."

"I see."

Tell me something: Does this country really need a bunch of accountants, advertising executives, and go-go dancers who know how to perform open heart surgery?

I don't think so.

Once upon a time, in my long-distant childhood, staying home and watching television was the social equivalent of minding your own business. Lucy got stuck on a window ledge. Beaver Cleaver went to the park and got his head stuck in a wrought-iron fence.

No blood.

No -ectomies.

Bliss.

Today, you can watch married couples thrash out their differences on *Geraldo* and then switch over to cable, just in time to see somebody's vas deferens get snipped.

In my suddenly manic state I wanted to rush across the room and rip the cable out of the wall.

I didn't, of course, but you can imagine how surprised I was to find out, the very next day, that "vasectomy" is Latin for "rip the cable out of the wall."

Learning things is so educational.

Flash from Mars

What a difference a meteorite makes.

On Saturday afternoon I was on the couch, bored stiff, flicking the channels, ready for a nap, when all of a sudden, I come upon Buster Crabbe saying, "Remember, Dale … we're on Mars!"

Mars?

I knew immediately that I was watching *The Deadly Ray from Mars* (the movie version of the serial *Flash Gordon's Trip to Mars*) and I was really happy because: Mars is so hot right now; I love Flash Gordon movies; and I love *any* movies that have lines like "Remember, Dale … we're on Mars."

When I was a kid I wanted *desperately* to be Flash Gordon, because I knew he had an exciting life. I mean, really: When you have to stop every so often to remind your friends what planet you're on, chances are you don't stay home much.

And Mars! The red planet! Hot, hot, hot.

So now I have to get some popcorn and watch the *whole* thing, because I've been looking at this Martian rock all week long, and reading all these headlines about life on Mars because someone found a rock—"a meteorite the size of a baked potato," according to the wire stories—with fossilized bacteria in it.

Whoa! Bacteria!

I can still remember how enthused, confused, and excited I was when one of those first newsbreaks came on Channel 4 and Sue Simmons smiled and said "Life on Mars! Story at eleven!"

Well, *my* ears perked right up: Life on Mars? There's *life* on Mars?

And I started jumping up and down a little because—you know—this is a big story. But then I started to wonder. I mean, I love Sue Simmons, I think she's the cutest thing going, but she isn't exactly Walter Cronkite. I'm sure if someone held up a card that said, "Porky Pig ate the president today," she'd just read it without batting an eyelash.

So, anyway, I watched all this stuff on the rock and, I have to be honest with you, it wasn't *that* exciting. I mean, I just always assumed bacteria were everywhere. Certainly, they're everywhere at my house. But everyone else in the country seemed happy about it, so I was happy for them.

And now it's a few days later and I'm watching Flash Gordon running around Mars, and it's funny because I haven't seen this thing in years, but I remember it so vividly.

So there's Flash and his girlfriend, Dale Arden, and over there is Dr. Zarkov with Happy and Prince Barin, and they're all talking with the Clay People, who Queen Azura turned into Martian rocks—now there's a coincidence—using the mysterious Black Sapphire of Kalu.

To hell with bacteria.

Then there's this flashback to when Flash met Prince Barin in *Flash Gordon Conquers the Universe.*

In order to gain his freedom, Flash had to fight Barin while Ming the Merciless watched with his daughter Princess Allura (no relation to Queen Azura), Dale Arden (who screams through the whole thing), and this really jolly old guy, who's the king of the Hawk People, or the prince of the Hawk People, or the president, or something.

I remembered all of this, too, because I thought the Hawk People were really cool because they had these big hooked noses, like all my mother's cousins, and these huge flapping wings coming out of their back.

Anyway, once the flashback is finished, we see Flash promising the leader of the Clay People that he, Dale, Zarkov, Happy, and Barin are all going to head out to the forest because they think the Black Sapphire has been stolen by the Forest People—who actually had it *first,* before Queen Azura stole it from *them.*

So Flash and the gang head out to the forest in a stolen spaceship—Mars is obviously a high crime planet—and, of course, they all split up, and, of course, the Forest People capture Dale, who for some reason is wearing a black sequined evening gown.

Hey, you're going to Mars, you pack a few things.

The Forest People then take Dale to the Temple of Kalu, where the High Priest forces her to breathe the Incense of Forgetfulness, and commands her to defend the Temple against all interlopers.

So, of course, the next thing you know, Flash comes to rescue her, but she has forgotten who he is, who she is, where they are, and which way is up. For some reason, however, she has not forgotten to defend the temple against interlopers, so she picks up the Silver Dagger of Kalu and stabs Flash in the back.

This really annoyed me, because it was Flash who took her to Mars in the first place. She never would have gotten there otherwise.

On the other hand, I do know how women can get when they're on vacation, because when I was a kid and we'd go away to the mountains, I remember my mother used to crack up a little too. She'd whine, and complain, and say she wanted to go home, and stuff like that.

But she never stabbed my father in the back with the Silver Dagger of the Poconos because, quite honestly, he never would have stood for it.

Now I'm *really* excited with all this intense drama going on, but it turns out that I'm not watching the movie version of the serial; I'm watching the serial version of the serial. And that's the end of it, and I can't see any more until next week. And I'm totally crestfallen.

On the other hand, I'm grateful for the bit of it that I did see and happy that they didn't make a movie about Flash Gordon going to Mars and finding bacteria, because bacteria don't speak English, and bacteria hardly ever wear evening gowns, and because, frankly, that wouldn't have been nearly as realistic.

The Cookie Lady

It's a quarter to three and there's no one in the place except Debbi Fields. And me.

Actually, Debbi hasn't even arrived yet. I'm sitting in my living room, after a long night, and switching channels. (At 3 A.M. there isn't a whole lot to choose from.) There's half a chicken pot pie warming in the oven and someone on the food channel is telling me to stay tuned for *Hospitality* with Debbi Fields.

Do you get the food channel? Have you ever seen Debbi Fields? She is this terribly attractive woman who is forever making desserts—cookies, pies, cupcakes—and forever drizzling chocolate on everything she touches.

"Let's drizzle some chocolate on this!" she says. "Doesn't that look *nice?*"

Either that or she's stuffing everything with Reese's peanut butter cups.

"The kids will just *love* these!" she insists. "Don't they look *pretty?*"

When I was a kid, if I had ever asked my mother to make a cake filled with Reese's peanut butter cups, she would have whacked me with her rolling pin.

At any rate, Ms. Debbi has apparently expanded her horizons from newfangled desserts to good old hospitality. In either milieu, she's a scary figure. Too pretty to be in the kitchen all day long. Too sweet and perky to be for real.

By the stroke of three my pot pie still wasn't done but there was Debbi—big eyes, big teeth, Godzilla-length fingernails—oohing and cooing about throwing together some back-to-school bash for the kids. (The premise: School can be a lonely place. Let your child invite everyone from his or her class—all thirty of them—to a party at your house, so everyone can become friends!)

My parents never threw me a back-to-school bash—although when I turned sixteen and told my father I didn't want to go back to school, he bashed my head in. (Does that count?)

I stuck with Debbi for the whole half hour and there were times I became so frightened I had to pull a blanket over my head. With her manic devotion to homemade crafts and do-it-yourself goodies, Debbi makes Martha Stewart ("I can't talk now. I'm making peach cobbler ...") look like Leona Helmsley ("I can't talk now. I'm kicking the servants ...").

Instead of traditional Hallmark-style invitations (total cost: about $5 for thirty), Debbi suggested that you buy some small blackboards and turn *them* into your invitations. Just write all the information on them in washable paint, wrap them in brightly colored tissue, and put them in lunch bags, with boxes of colored chalk. (Include a note to the mothers explaining that the paint is washable and that the blackboards can be used for all sorts of fun activities.) Then you take some red construction paper, cut out little paper apples, apply them to the bags with your glue stick—You do have a glue stick, don't you?— and let your kid bring them to school and hand them out to everyone in the class. (Total cost: about $645.)

At no point does Debbi explain how your child is supposed to carry thirty lunch bags filled with blackboards and chalk to class— *"Load him up like a pack mule!"*—although she does offer an alternative: mailing the blackboards in envelopes lined with bubble wrap. (Just add another $60 for the envelopes and postage.)

That out of the way, Debbi explained her menu: ABC Sandwiches, Teacher's Pet Pasta Salad, Time-Out Tortilla Chips, and Back-to-School Brownies. (Just between us, I think Debbi's been hitting the Prozac Pizza Squares again.)

The ABC in the ABC sandwiches, incidentally, stands for apples, bananas, and cheese—which sent me screaming from the room.

Does *anyone* actually do stuff like this?

All of the food should be made ahead of time, says Debbi, The Good Mom, so you can have more time at the party to spend with the children. (Yeah, right. If my mother had thirty kids running around her house, she'd lock herself in the bathroom and wouldn't come out until she'd swallowed every tranquilizer in the medicine cabinet.)

The sandwiches, tortilla chips, and brownies go in little plastic storage bags; the salads go in little plastic containers; and the whole party lunch winds up being put in individual insulated lunch bags—preferably the cloth ones with zippers. (And what's *that* going to cost? The woman has completely lost her mind.)

Debbi also suggested putting little notes in with the sandwiches—catch me, I'm falling—and insisted she does this every day with her own children's lunches. ("I always put a message in their sandwich like, 'Oh! You're special!'")

My mother never put messages in my school lunches, although I used to plead with her to give me "normal" food, because all the other kids would be eating Taylor ham on Wonder bread, and I'd show up with eggplant parmigiana heroes, or squash and eggs, and everyone thought I came from the planet Retardo.

For "party fun" Debbi suggested giving the kids colored sidewalk chalk and letting them "run wild" in the driveway. (I don't personally recommend this unless the children are younger than eighteen months or you're prepared to stand on the roof all day with a machine gun.) After which, she said, they can make papier-mâché animals and decorate them with acrylic paints and Magic Markers.

"Of course this can be a little messy," she explained, "but it's so much fun!"

(For whom? The dry cleaner?)

Your back-to-school bash will bring your child's class closer together and allow him or her to make lasting friendships. "I know that when I first went to school," Debbi said, "I felt completely abandoned." (I knew if I watched her long enough, I'd find out what was wrong with her.)

Debbi, dear ... listen to me: Trim those nails, stop smiling so much, ditch the Reese's peanut butter cups, take some time off, and work all of this out with a professional. When you're done, come back to television with some shows on useful subjects, like how to keep other people's children out of your house and how to remove papier-mâché from the coffee table.

I know you can do it.

I believe in you.

You're special.

At Home with the Yule Log

The Yule Log stretches out comfortably on a well-worn sofa in his small New Jersey home. The place is cozy, but hardly the kind of digs you'd expect a big-time television star to own.

"The fact is," Yule says, sipping a Perrier, "I'm not a big-time star anymore. I guess you can thank WPIX for that."

There is a trace of bitterness in his voice. His expression is blank. Wooden.

Like so many Amercians, the Yule Log, a staple on local TV for a decade, is out of work. And it hurts, he says.

"I still have a knot in my stomach," he tells me. "I have one on my shoulder too."

Two years ago, WPIX axed his Christmas Eve show titled, simply, *The Yule Log*. It was the end of an era. No longer could those of us without fireplaces turn on the tube and see an old friend blazing away.

"And do you think they even sent me a card?" he crackles. "Of course not. They're cruel, I tell ya. No, worse than cruel. They're … they're …"

Hearthless?

He turns away, takes another slug of Perrier, and composes himself.

"I loved that job," he pines. "But what are you gonna do? These days everything is ratings, ratings, ratings. It's insane. No matter what anybody tells you, this is a wicked business, especially if you're a log. We have no union, you know. No protection. It's so easy to get burned."

He says he still has a few friends in the business.

"Joe Franklin calls every so often, bless his heart. He's had me on the show a few times, and he always makes me feel good. No matter what anyone tells you, he's a gentleman. He has respect for stars who are—How should I put it?—between engagements. And he still gets interesting guests. The last time I was on, he also had Garbo's astrologer and the official spokesman for the tomato industry."

He shifts uncomfortably in his seat. "Anyway, that's how it goes in this business. One day you're on the top of the pile. The next day, your résumés are coming back unopened. 'Return to Cinder.'"

He takes another sip of his water. "My agent hasn't even called me since the *Twin Peaks* debacle. The bum. I was up for the part of the Log Lady's log. I don't know if you remember reading about that in *Variety*."

I tell him I must have missed it. "Was it a nice story?"

"Hey, look," he laughs, "publicity is publicity. But I really would have loved that part. David Lynch [the series creator] has a wonderful eye. And, of course, the log was a central part. But as you know, I didn't get it. He whittled it down to three of us and then … what can you do? I had my trunk packed and everything.

I ask if he's done series work before.

"Oh, sure," he replies. "Back in the sixties I got plenty of work over at CBS. *The Beverly Hillbillies, Green Acres, Petticoat Junction* … they had all those rural shows back then. It was great. I had some wonderful parts. Came this close to an Emmy nomination. And then, of course, there was *Little House on the Prairie*. I worked steadily for seven years."

I make the mistake of asking who he played on *Little House on the Prairie*.

"You don't do your homework, do you kid? I played the house, dammit."

His most recent role was in a cheap, made-for-TV thriller playing, of all things, a houseplant. "Yeah," he smirks, "they covered me with leaves and had me sitting in the corner. I was onscreen for four or five seconds, but it was a paycheck. Besides, there are no small roles, only small logs."

Did it hurt that no one recognized him? "Actually, that's not true," he says. "I got a mention in the *Times*. They said I had matured into character roles. Made it look like I was branching out, so to speak. I thought that was awfully nice of them. And let's face it, I am pushing seventy, and there's a whole new crop out there. The woods are full of 'em."

I tell him he looks much, much younger.

"Well, I take care of myself," he says. "Plenty of fiber. But I am sixty-eight years old. If you don't believe me you can count the rings."

I decline and remind him of all his fans who are going to miss him this Christmas Eve.

"I know, I know," he says. "I get their cards all the time—on recycled paper, bless their hearts. Please, tell them I miss them too. I hope they all have a wonderful holiday. And I'll be back; you'll see. One thing a log knows how to do is roll with it."

The End of the World

It's Wednesday night. My parents have just watched a television special on the end of the world.

They're not happy about it.

So my mother calls at 8:30 all upset. I was sprawled out on the couch at this point, dog tired, already drifting off to sleep.

"Hi, what's new?" she asked.

Even though I was half asleep I could tell right away that something was wrong—just by that funny quaver in her voice. *Oh, crud.* I hope my father isn't in the backyard barking at the Chinese people's dog again.

"Nothing much," I told her, trying to stifle a yawn. "What's new over there?"

"Well, I don't know," she said. "I'm not going to say we're bent into shape or anything …"

"Bent *out* of shape," I corrected her, eyelids drooping back down.

"Whatever. But we just watched this show on the end of the world. And, frankly, I'm a little concerned."

"I see."

Do they really have to put on shows like this at 8 o'clock, when impressionable senior citizens are still awake?

"They say it's coming," she added. "It's in all these books, plus it's in the Bible, and all these scientists are saying the same thing. And they say everything points to the next few years."

"Really?"

"Yes. And they're not kidding. It was just on Channel Two. Your father saw it too."

I'm nodding now like a psychiatrist, trying to get into my rational mode. When parents get all upset like this, it's best to treat their fear seriously and then walk them through it.

"Ma," I said softly, "I'm sleeping. What do you *want?*"

"Well," she said, "your father and I got to talking and we were just wondering: If the world was really coming to an end, you'd come *home,* wouldn't you?"

Never mind that I moved out twenty-one years ago. I'm sure that Barbra Streisand—who owns something like seven houses and a forty-three-room apartment in Manhattan—still gets calls from her mother asking, "Are you coming *home* on Sunday? Your cousin Shirley's stopping over."

I told my mother that in the face of imminent doom I'd most likely stay put. Besides, the traffic going out to Long Island is bad enough when the world *isn't* coming to an end. If stars were falling out of the sky and the earth was cracking open, I'm sure the expressway would be bumper to bumper.

She started telling me something else, then covered the phone and screamed *"No!"* at my father. Putting the receiver back to her mouth she said, "That was your stupid father! He keeps yelling at me to make the coffee!"

"It's already eight thirty," I told her. "You still haven't made the coffee?"

"No," she said. "What's the point?"

"Ma, look," I said, "this sort of thing has been going on forever. People always think the world is going to end in their lifetime. And it never has."

"That's not true," she told me.

Oh, here we go. Tell me I *missed* it.

"They're saying now that the dinosaurs were all killed when this big comet hit the earth. It must've been going—I don't know—two hundred miles an hour. And then there was the Great Flood. That thing killed everybody too. And then I think there was something else; I can't remember."

Is there any way *out* of this conversation?

"OK, look," I said, finally, "if they found out the world was coming to an end, and there was enough time, I'd definitely drive out there to be with you and Dad. Who else could I possibly want to be with?"

I could tell she was pleased. "You could even leave the night before," she advised me. "Beat the traffic."

"Good idea."

"Well, all right," she said. "If you're coming out next week we can show you that program; your father taped it."

My eyes suddenly shot open.

"Excuse me?"

"I said your father taped the program."

My father?

My father taped something?

On the VCR?

"Yeah," she said. "After six years he finally figured out how to do it. Isn't that something?"

Oh my God.

The world is coming to an end.

I Love Lucy

Every couple of months or so I wake up, turn on *I Love Lucy,* and see the Ricardos and the Mertzes heading off for Hollywood—one more time—in their pretty new Pontiac convertible.

Lucy and Ricky are sitting up front. Fred and Ethel, holding up the rear, join in a chorus of "California, Here I Come."

That particular episode first aired in January of 1955, six months before I was born. And I suspect it will continue to run long after I'm dead and buried, next to my word processor, under a stone that says "I'm on deadline. Come back tomorrow."

As it is, I'm already graying, wrinkling, and wondering where the time has gone. But the Ricardos and the Mertzes just keep driving out to California and coming back again, sailing off to Europe and coming back again, moving out to Connecticut and coming back again, in black-and-white, time-warping perpetuity.

Thirty-seven years later, these images remain crisp and familiar—constants in a world where nothing else stays the same. And they occurred to me again last weekend on one of my periodic visits to Long Island.

On these mileage-crammed Sundays, I generally drive from town to town—like Richard Simmons with his Deal-a-Meal cards—stopping in on friends and relatives and telling them all how great they look.

Wherever I go, there's generally a tall glass of ice water waiting for me—the taller the better—and a television blaring somewhere in the house.

My first stop on Sunday was to see my friend Bob, whom I've known for seventeen years. When he first became ill, I promised myself I'd try to visit him every other week. And I've kept the promise.

While I'm there Bob generally lies on the couch with his white cat sleeping on his chest and the black one nearby, stretched out under the coffee table. One is named Pookie and the other is

Marvin, but I still don't know which is which. I wander into the kitchen, get my glass of ice water, and we watch something on TV.

Last week it was *When the Lion Roared,* the TBS documentary on the golden age of MGM. Bob's only forty-one, but he's always been a fan of old movies, and he seemed to get a kick out of seeing the classic film clips and the interviews with the stars.

He interrupted their anecdotes with stories of his own—things he had read in movie books or magazines—and we laughed for an hour and a half.

As I sat there staring at the screen, I couldn't help but think of all the times we've watched television together through the years, at his house or my house or wherever else we happened to be. I thought of our old buddy Scott who moved to Florida in 1983; of my great friend Carol, who married some cop and lost touch with all of us; of John "The Fish," who gave up his fish business a few years ago and became a construction supervisor for some refrigeration outfit in the city.

John sends his regards, by the way. We still keep in touch. And Scott's coming up next month for a few days. Everybody knows Bob is dying. Even Bob. But we never talk about it.

My next stop was Massapequa Park to see my friend Rich, his sister Danielle, and their parents, Alice and Bernie. I've known them for so long too.

Rich, who's my age, tells me he's going through some "personal stuff" right now. He's staying with his folks for a month or so and then he's moving to Queens. He needs a job, but there aren't any, although he knows someone who knows someone else who might have something for him. Danielle, twenty-one, is getting married soon—I still can't believe it—and Alice and Bernie are talking about moving down south.

God, I never thought they'd leave that house.

Their kitchen is a bright space, despite all that paneling, and tons of early Americana. Their Siamese cat China died a couple of years ago. They have a new one now, and she looks just like the old one. Same coloring and everything.

Behind me as I sipped my water was a twelve-inch TV on a plain wooden stand, and *Bonnie and Clyde* was screaming in my ear. We eventually lowered the sound, but no one turned off the set.

It was a nice visit. We laughed a lot. Occasionally, we'd catch ourselves staring at the screen. The Oscars were on the following night and I doubted out loud that Warren Beatty was going to win for *Bugsy*.

Last stop was to see my parents. I had told them I wasn't going to be eating with them, but my mother had something waiting for me anyway. Dad was in the den in some big, new easy chair, snoring in front of the tube. Mom was putting glasses in the dishwasher and telling me about a lamp shade she'd bought, with a blue frill to match the couch.

Seemed like old times. And as I chowed down, I got the latest on this one and that one, who got a promotion, which relatives aren't feeling well, and which ones are "going for tests."

Dad woke up, suddenly, jarred by the TV. He looks so old when he wakes up like that. He's got a great smile, though. And the first thing he did was reach out to shake my hand.

I left before dusk, heading west on the Southern State Parkway, watching the sky slowly redden, then blacken around me.

That's when I thought of the Ricardos, their trip to California, and they're pretty new convertible.

I fumbled through my pocket to find money for the tolls, turned on the radio, and hummed along to pass the time.

And when I could, I looked over at the drivers on either side of me and wondered, just for a moment, what their lives were like.

About the Author

Bill Ervolino is a columnist and entertainment writer for the *Record*, a daily newspaper in northern New Jersey. In 1994, Ervolino received the top prize for his humor column from the Society of Silurians, the country's oldest journalism group. He also is a two-time finalist in the Penney-Missouri feature-writing competition. Ervolino has been an entertainment writer and critic for the *New York Post* and columnist for *Backstage,* and has written for *Entertainment Weekly, Vogue,* and *Parent's Choice.* In 1987, his play, "The Lights on Walden Court," won the first Jane Chambers Playwriting Award.